WALKS FOR ALL AGES
HEREFORDSHIRE

WALKS *FOR* ALL **AGES**

HEREFORDSHIRE

HEREFORDSHIRE RAMBLERS

BRADWELL
BOOKS

Published by Bradwell Books
9 Orgreave Close Sheffield S13 9NP
Email: books@bradwellbooks.co.uk

1st Edition
Reprinted 2019

ISBN: 9781902674995

Print: CPI Group (UK) Ltd, Croydon CR0 4YY

Design by: Erik Siewko Creative, Derbyshire.
eriksiewko@gmail.com

Photograph Credits: © Members of The Herefordshire Ramblers 2014
Except pages 57, 77, 94 & 95, supplied by Visit Herefordshire
and front cover © shutterstock David Hughes

Maps: Contain Ordnance Survey data
© Crown copyright and database right 2014

Ordnance Survey licence number 100039353

The information in this book has been produced in good faith and is intended as a general guide. Bradwell Books and its authors have made all reasonable efforts to ensure that the details are correct at the time of publication. Bradwell Books and the author cannot accept any responsibility for any changes that have taken place subsequent to the book being published. It is the responsibility of individuals undertaking any of the walks listed in this publication to exercise due care and consideration for the health and wellbeing of each other in the party. Particular care should be taken if you are inexperienced. The walks in this book are not especially strenuous but individuals taking part should ensure they are fit and able to complete the walk before setting off.

Various walks in this book have been marked with the Dog Friendly Logo; a stamp of approval identifying the walk as suitable for your canine companions.
The maps are drawn to different scales but each grid square represents one kilometre.

INTRODUCTION

HEREFORDSHIRE IS ONE OF THE LEAST POPULATED COUNTIES OF ENGLAND – AND ALSO ONE OF THE LEAST KNOWN. THAT IS GOOD NEWS FOR THE WALKER, BECAUSE WHEREVER YOU ARE IN HEREFORDSHIRE, THE COUNTRYSIDE IS NEVER FAR AWAY, AND THE CONCEPT OF HONEYPOTS DOESN'T REALLY APPLY!

These walks make full use of the wonderful variety of walking in Herefordshire. We range from the woods of Wigmore (walk 1), through the black-and-white villages, like Weobley (walk 20), the Black Mountains (walk 19), the stunning Wye Valley (walks 2, 4 and 16) to the distinctive market towns of Bromyard (walk 5), Ledbury (walk 14), Kington (walk 12) and Ross-on-Wye (walks 17 and 18). Two walks (2 and 10) are very close to the centre of Hereford.

Mostly we follow public rights of way or walk over open access land. We have included some well-established permissive paths which have been walked for many years. There is also some country lane walking, one of the delights of Herefordshire, and very short distances on bigger roads. Do please take care on roads, especially with children or dogs.

Many of us like to take our dogs with us on walks. These walks are generally extremely dog-friendly in that there are few stiles, so most dogs will be able to complete all the walks in this book. Dogs should, however, be always under control and on leads on lanes and in the vicinity of sheep, cattle and ponies.

HEREFORDSHIRE IS RENOWNED FOR THE VARIETY OF ITS LOCALLY PRODUCED FOOD, SO WE HOPE YOU WILL ENJOY THE HOSPITALITY.
A NUMBER OF PUBS ARE HAPPY TO WELCOME DOGS, AND WE MENTION SOME OF THEM.

However, for many of the walks dogs can be off the lead for most of the time. We assess each walk for its dog-friendliness.

We have taken great care over the accuracy of the walk description and the map, but things do change on the ground over time; for instance stiles may get replaced by gates. The relevant 1:25000 (Explorer or Outdoor Leisure range) Ordnance Survey map is useful back-up. If you find any obstructions to your route it would be very helpful to report the problem to Herefordshire Council. You can email them on streets@herefordshire.gov.uk.

Enjoy your walking in Herefordshire.

WIGMORE STANDS ON THE SOUTH-WESTERN EDGE OF A BROAD VALLEY THAT WAS A GLACIAL LAKE AT THE END OF THE ICE AGE.

It was of strategic importance at the time of the Norman Conquest, lying between the River Teme to the north and the River Lugg to the south. The highlight of this wonderful walk is undoubtedly the 11th-century Wigmore Castle. The castle is now a spectacular ruin (deliberately destroyed by its owner in the Civil War) but in its day was of immense historical significance, being the home of the Mortimers, the most powerful of the Marcher lords. You can visit the castle free of charge: indeed you can only visit on foot!

The first part of the walk gives lovely views across the valley followed by a pretty country lane. The return is along a broad pine forest track to Adforton.

Wigmore Castle is one of the most spectacular and historically important sites in Herefordshire. From shortly after the Norman Conquest until the early 15th century, Wigmore was home to the powerful Mortimer family. Lords of the Welsh Marches, as the Mortimers were, had many special privileges, including the right to make war, to hold courts, and to receive tax revenues. In 1329, Roger Mortimer held a lavish tournament at Wigmore, attended by the young King Edward III and his mother, Queen Isabella, who was also Roger's lover. In 1327 Roger and

Isabella deposed Edward II in favour of the young Edward III, then aged 14. But in 1330 Edward III asserted his independence, arrested Mortimer and had him executed for treason. Wigmore later passed to the Harley family. In the Civil War the Parliamentarian Harleys were unable to defend both Wigmore and their main home at nearby Brampton Bryan, so they demolished large parts of Wigmore. The castle is now under the care of English Heritage. It is free, open all year round, has spectacular views, and is an ideal place for a summer picnic.

THE BASICS

Distance: 4 miles (6½ km)

Gradient: Moderate

Severity: Moderate

Approx time to walk: 2½ hours

Stiles: Three

Maps: OS Explorer 201 (Knighton and Presteigne) and 203 (Ludlow)

Start Point: Adforton church: SO402711; SY7 0ND

Parking: Car park next to church

Dog friendly: Yes – an excellent walk for dogs

Public Toilets: Wigmore

Nearest food: Wigmore: The Castle Inn; Leintwardine: Lion, Sun inns, fish and chip shop

ADFORTON TO WIGMORE CASTLE

1. Walk up the lane away from the main road. In 50 metres at the end of the lane, ignore the bridle path ahead and turn left into a green lane. Follow this lane uphill through a metal gate, then immediately turn left. Continue through the next gate and turn right to a stile at the entrance to a wood. Enjoy the views to the east of Leinthall Starkes and Elton. Follow this woodland path to a clearing and forest road coming in from the right.

2. Bear left along a forest path and continue for just under a mile (approximately 1.25 km) to a wooden gate marking the end of the forest path. Continue downhill through open scrub. Keep right onto an incoming path from the left. Keep to this path on the edge of the wood to a wooden gate. Continue to the entrance to Wigmore Castle.

3. Turn left down steps away from the castle. Go through double kissing gates and turn right following the fence line to a metal gate into a field. Follow an indistinct path up a field with the hedge and tree line on your left. Continue to the top far corner. (This part can become overgrown and it may be necessary to divert to the right to get round to the stile in the top corner). Go over the stile and continue in the same direction along the field edge with bracken on your right. After approximately 200 metres turn left at the free-standing stile, then walk over a field to another stile and onto the road. Turn right along the road. Bear left down the hill. At the bottom of the hill continue over a small bridge and, as you go up hill, in approximately 100 metres turn right onto a wide forest road.

4. Keep on this main forest road, ignoring any tracks to the left or right, enjoying the views through the clearings of the Shropshire hills to the north. In just over half a mile (approximately 1 km) go round some double bends. At these bends again ignore tracks coming in from the right and left, keeping to the main forest road. Continue uphill to a Y junction. Take the right-hand fork, again keeping

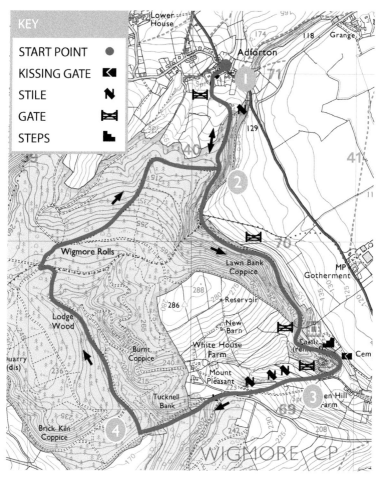

KEY

START POINT ●

KISSING GATE ◖

STILE Ν

GATE ⋈

STEPS ∟

to the main forest road. After approximately 700 metres you will come to the clearing you encountered near to the start of the walk (2). Turn left along the woodland path, retracing your steps to the car park at Adforton.

BREINTON

THE CITY OF HEREFORD HAS A GREAT DEAL TO OFFER. IT
IS AN ATTRACTIVE CITY WITH ITS PICTURESQUE RIVERBANK
AND MANY EXAMPLES OF BEAUTIFUL PERIOD ARCHITECTURE.

The city's rich heritage can be seen from its extraordinary
relics from bygone days, most notably the spectacular
Norman Cathedral, the Mappa Mundi maps and the
Chained Library exhibition. There is also a cider museum,
which is particularly relevant to this walk. Hereford has
excellent shopping facilities and a great range of cafes,
restaurants and pubs.

This walk combines a delightful stroll in the Wye Valley with some bird-spotting, two
managed woodlands and many echoes of Herefordshire's proud history of cider-making
– all within a stone's throw of the middle of Hereford.

THE WALK.

1.   From your car make your way towards the car park entrance and take the stile on the left and go over another stile, turn to the right and cross a stile to the main A438 road. (These are three fairly easy and dog-friendly stiles but you can avoid them all by simply walking out through the main entrance and turning left on the main road). Carefully cross this road and turn left and walk on the pavement towards Hereford until you reach the Bay Horse Inn.

2.   Turn right onto a bridleway and follow the hedge on your right to a pedestrian gate into Millennium Wood also known as Drovers Wood (now managed by the Woodland Trust but formerly owned by Gillian Bulmer of the Bulmer cider-making family). Follow the hedge on the right to come out of the wood onto a lane. This is Green Lane and was a drovers' road along which huge herds of Welsh cattle passed en route to Hereford and London. The drovers stayed overnight at an area called the King's Acre, where there was a drinking pond for the animals. Turn right and then left along a lane until you reach a country road.

THE BASICS

Distance: 4½ miles (7 km)

Gradient: Two gentle climbs

Severity: Easy

Approx time to walk: 2 ½ hours

Stiles: Four or one

Maps: OS Explorer 189: Hereford and Ross-on-Wye

Path description: Tarmac lanes and grassy footpaths

Start Point: Wyevale Garden Centre: SO471416; HR4 0SE

Parking: Park at far end of car park

Dog Friendly: Yes, the stiles are dog friendly but dogs will need to be on leads on the lanes

Public Toilets: Wyevale Garden Centre

Nearest food: Wyevale Garden Centre, Bay Horse Inn

3. Turn left on the road, looking out for the cider press on your right. Turn right at the first turning to come to a crossroads at Warham Farm. Turn right and immediately left to follow the road passing the drive to Wareham House to reach a footpath on the right.

4. Go through the pedestrian gate and follow the hedge on your right, noticing the Green Bank information board. Stay close to Warham House (ignore the path off to your left) to reach a metal kissing gate. Turn right through the kissing gate and then immediately left. Keep left following the hedge on your left. At another kissing gate you enter  a strip of woodland, where you will see bluebells in the spring and a glimpse of the Wye below. On reaching a further kissing gate, you arrive at Breinton Church on your right. Go through the lych gate into the churchyard where you can enjoy the surroundings on a bench and perhaps listen to some birdsong.

5. Duly rested, leave the churchyard via the same gate and go slightly to the right to a pedestrian gate on the right into the orchard. Go diagonally left through the orchard to a kissing gate. Go through this gate and, before you go through a metal gate on the opposite side of the lane, you might like to admire the magnificent beasts at the gate of Breinton House. Follow the stone path to the gate ahead and then on grass to a gate in a hedge on  the right. Go through a gate and up a drive with a house on your right to a kissing gate. Through the gate, proceed straight ahead with the hedge on your right, ignoring the path on the left until you reach a large farm gate (which will open) with an awkward stile to its left. Keep going ahead with the hedge on the right to cross a stile into a quiet lane. Cross the lane and proceed straight ahead on the footpath opposite, a fence now on your left, until you reach a crossroads of paths.

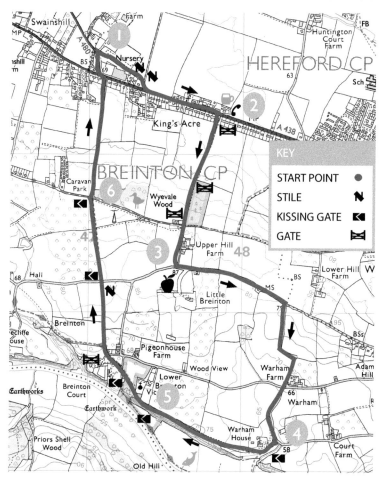

KEY

START POINT	●
STILE	↰
KISSING GATE	◄
GATE	⋈

6.   Go straight ahead alongside Wyevale Wood on the right. Woodpeckers flourish here, as they do in the many orchards around Breinton. Percy and Fred Bulmer launched their legendary Woodpecker cider brand in 1896. The Bulmers came from nearby Credenhill, so we can imagine them listening to the woodpeckers in orchards and woods like these. There is more information at the Cider Museum in Hereford. Continue until you come to the main A438 road with Wyevale Garden Centre opposite. Cross carefully and go to the right into the garden centre for a well-earned cup of tea.

BRINGSTY COMMON

BRINGSTY COMMON, FOUR MILES (6.5 KM) EAST OF
BROMYARD, IS ONE OF HEREFORDSHIRE'S BEST-LOVED
GEMS.

It consists of 300 acres of common land which provides a diverse environment for a range of wildlife including the muntjac, the redwing and the merlin. The extensive bracken is home to the caterpillar of the rare high brown fritillary butterfly. As a common, it is designated as access land under the Countryside and Rights of Way Act 2000 and you can walk anywhere except in private gardens. So feel free to choose your own route and enjoy the Common.

This walk is simply a suggestion to include some of the best bits. There are extensive views in all directions and it is a particularly good walk for dogs, especially if they like meeting other dogs! It is quite possible to get slightly lost (even with these directions!) but do not worry. A familiar landmark will soon appear to help you regain your bearings.

THE BASICS

Distance: 3 miles (5 km)

Gradient: One gentle ascent

Severity: Easy

Approx time to walk: 1½ hours

Stiles: None

Maps: OS Explorers 202 (Leominster and Bromyard) and 204 (Worcester and Droitwich Spa)

Path description: Grass or stone tracks. The grass tracks can get muddy in winter.

Start Point: Small parking area just off A44 at the mouth of the track to the Live & Let Live, Bringsty Common: SO700548; WR6 5UW

Parking: As above

Dog friendly: This is the ideal walk for dogs. They can come into the pub too!

Public Toilets: None

Nearest food: Live & Let Live, Bringsty Common; Bringsty Cafe

BRINGSTY COMMON WALK

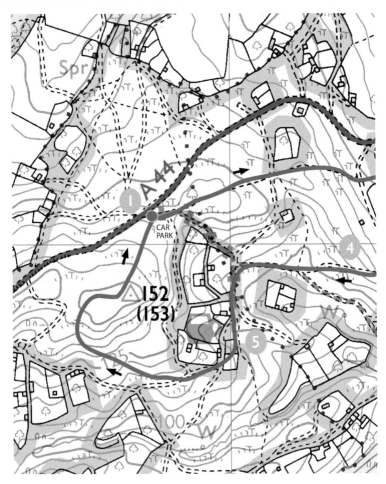

1. From the parking area, go down the track and after 50 metres turn left on a grass path where you will see the magnificent Gospel Oak, marking the boundary between Whitbourne and Linton parishes. It is called Gospel Oak because on Rogation Sunday it was traditional to beat the bounds of the parish and read the gospel from this spot. Carry on along the grass path to a clearing with newly planted fruit trees and a spaghetti junction of paths. Bear half-left (the second 'exit') and you soon drop down steeply to a stone track. Turn right, then left at the notice across what used to be a cricket pitch and then along a broad grass track which winds its way through bracken to a stone turning circle. To the left there is a good view of Whitbourne Hall. Whitbourne Hall, with its imposing Greek-style facade, was built by Edward Evans, a millionaire who had made his money in vinegar, in 1861.

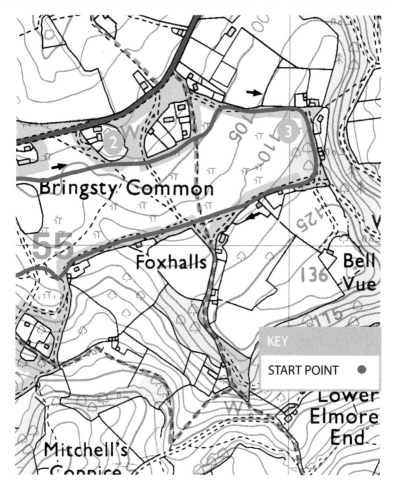

KEY

START POINT ●

2. Turn right and after 50 metres take the middle of three paths along a tree-covered path to another stone track. Go straight across and follow the path through some trees to a yellow bungalow (this is due to be rebuilt). Keep to the left of the common, then at some garages turn half-right to pass an electricity pole. At another stone track turn right. This track takes you through some trees and swings right past Cop Castle and Brackenberry.

3. Continue up the track, pausing to admire views of the Suckley hills on your left, and at Belvue turn sharp right past Holly Cottage and Brackentop. At the finger post you should notice 50 metres away the red telephone box which has mysteriously materialised in a front garden. Continue ahead straight across a stone track and continue along a grass track. After 250 metres bear right at the waymarker and you will soon reach a football pitch and a six-ways junction of paths.

4. Take the third 'exit' at 11 o'clock and head for the telegraph pole on the skyline. Admire the superb views of the Malverns to your left, before descending the reddish track with the pub clearly visible below. Head for the pub! The Live & Let Live is one of the oldest buildings on the common and dates from c.1700.

It was originally a cider house. Between the wars, Bringsty Common and Bromyard Downs were favourite destinations for cyclists from Birmingham, and groups of up to 40 or 50 used to cycle down on a Sunday to picnic and visit the Live & Let Live. The pub was empty from 2002 to 2007 but has been wonderfully restored and is now a great place for walkers, families and indeed anyone who enjoys real ale and real fish and chips in a beautiful setting. Dogs on leads are also welcome in the pub. You can of course easily start the walk from here, an excellent option if you want to enjoy a drink at the end of the walk.

5. Carry on past the pub car park and a cottage on your right to a pollarded willow. Bear right, keeping close to the trees on your right with another superb view of the Malverns to your left. After 50 metres from the willow, bear half-left parallel to the high ground on your right.

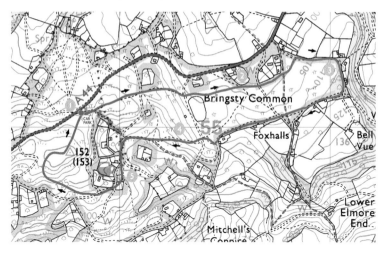

You could make a bee-line for the top here – this is common land so you can walk freely – but we will more sedately hold our straightish line on a grass path which will eventually wheel right. The path now climbs steeply and at a crossroads of paths turn right to the top of Bringsty Jubilee. Now you can enjoy the panoramic views from the viewfinder on top, west to Bromyard Downs, north-east to Abberley, east along the Teme Valley and south-east to the Malverns. If you have brought refreshments, this is the place to enjoy them. When it is time to move on, go straight ahead to a clump of trees and a trig point hidden amongst them and bear half-left down the hill to the notice board and car park.

BROCKHAMPTON & CAPLER

THE WALK STARTS AT ALL SAINTS' CHURCH, BROCKHAMPTON (PLEASE NOTE THAT THIS IS THE BROCKHAMPTON IN THE SOUTH OF THE COUNTY NEAR FOWNHOPE).

The thatched church and lychgate were completed in 1902, commissioned by Alice Foster of Brockhampton Court, nearby, in memory of her parents. The architect William Lethaby was a disciple of William Morris and the church is a wonderful example of Arts and Crafts design and workmanship. There is in a replica of the church in a skyscraper in Japan where weddings take place.

Brockhampton is in the Wye Valley Area of Outstanding Natural Beauty. From the Capler Viewpoint picnic site you will see a spectacular view through the ancient woodland to the river below. The entire course of the River Wye and its banks are designated as a Site of Special Scientific Interest.

At the top of the hill behind the viewpoint is Capler Camp, a large Iron Age hill-fort covering about 15 acres which was occupied from about 800 BC until AD 42. A short diversion is possible to view the hill-fort by walking up the track opposite the viewpoint.

THE BASICS

Distance: 2½ miles (4km)

Gradient: Slight

Severity: Easy

Approx time to walk: 1½ hours

Stiles: Seven

Maps: OS Explorer 189: Hereford and Ross-on-Wye

Path description: Field paths, green lanes, tracks and lanes

Start Point: Brockhampton Church: SO594321; HR1 4SE

Parking: Lay-by at Brockhampton Church

Dog friendly: There are some stiles and be aware there may be stock in some fields

Public Toilets: None

Nearest food: New Inn or Green man, Fownhope

1. Starting in front of the church, turn left and walk up the lane for a short distance. Pass Parks Pitch and turn left at the telephone kiosk onto a drive. Keep straight ahead and join a track continuing up to a cottage. Pass through the farm gate into a field and follow a diagonal path uphill to a stile in the hedge on the right. On top of the hill to your left you can see the site of Capler Camp, an ancient Iron Age hill-fort.

2. Cross the stile and continue on the diagonal path across the next field to another stile in the hedge. Turn around and enjoy a view of the Forest of Dean and May Hill, with its distinctive clump of trees. Go over the stile, turn left, keep the hedge on your left and cross another stile into the next field. Continue into another field, cross a stile and walk along the field edge. Leave along a track and cross the road to Capler Viewpoint and picnic site, slightly to the right. You have now joined the Wye Valley Walk long-distance footpath. Take a moment to rest on the installation provided by Brockhampton and Much Fawley Parish Council. This traces the line of the River Wye and the disused railway line and features images from local history and folklore. Also look through the trees to view a loop of the river.

3. Leave the viewpoint, turn right past a Wye Valley Walk information board and turn down a track to the right. Follow the track through woodland, go through a gate and pass West Cottage on your left. Continue to follow the track until you pass a group of cottages on the left.

4. As the track emerges onto a lane, turn right, then immediately left onto another track, continuing on the Wye Valley Walk, walking alongside a field. At the field corner turn left following a track, still on the Wye Valley Walk. Look out for a way marker on the right and at this point leave the track and the Wye Valley Walk, turn right and join a path, keeping the hedge to your left. Cross a stile, turn immediately left through a farm gate onto a track above a field. Walk through two more fields, enjoying

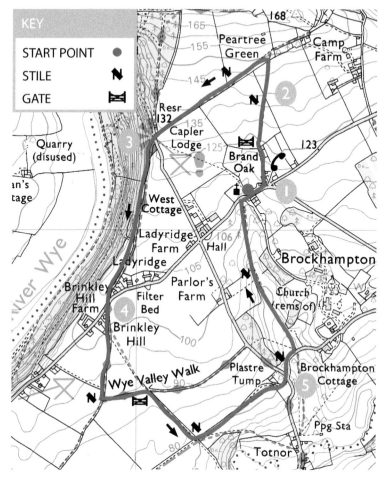

KEY

START POINT ●

STILE ⇖

GATE ⋈

168

165

155 Peartree Green

Camp Farm

145

Resr 132

135

Capler Lodge 125

Quarry (disused)

Brand Oak

123

West Cottage

Ladyridge Farm

106

Hall

Ladyridge 105

Parlor's Farm

Brockhampton

Brinkley Hill Farm

Filter Bed

Church (rems of)

Brinkley Hill

100

River Wye

Wye Valley Walk

90

Plastre Tump

Brockhampton Cottage

5

80

Ppg Sta

Totnor

a lovely view over Totnor and leave through another farm gate. Bear right along a track and go down to a crossroads.

5. At the crossroads keep straight ahead onto a lane going downhill. Look out for a fingerpost on the left and use the farm gate (please refasten) or stile to enter the field. Follow the path, gradually climbing from the valley bottom upwards through parkland. Cross an unusual stile or use the gate, and walk towards the church, leaving through a wrought iron gate. Take time to visit the beautiful Arts and Crafts church.

BROMYARD DOWNS

BROMYARD IS HEREFORDSHIRE'S MOST UNSPOILT MARKET TOWN AND OFFERS MUCH TO SEE AND TO DO. THE HIGH STREET IS STACKED WITH INTERESTING BLACK-AND-WHITE BUILDINGS, AND HAS AN ARRAY OF INDEPENDENT SHOPS, CAFES, PUBS AND BUSINESSES.

Bromyard is a town of festivals – hops, folk, marmalade, scarecrows, jazz, town criers – they all have their festival in Bromyard.

Bromyard is also a great place for walkers. Along with Kington, Leominster and Ross-on-Wye it has won official recognition as a town which welcomes walkers. And this is hardly surprising when you consider the opportunities on offer – the Frome Valley, delightful hamlets such as Thornbury, the heights of the Bromyard plateau,

the wilds of Bringsty Common (see walk 3 in this book) and of course, the jewel in the crown, Bromyard Downs.

Bromyard Downs is an exhilarating area of 800 acres of common land, which means you can walk anywhere (except through private gardens). Now you meet few people except for dog walkers but in the 19th century there was a racecourse on the Downs which attracted up to 7,000 people, many coming by train from Birmingham.

This walk will help you enjoy the Downs in all its beauty. Bromyard Downs contains wild meadows that are grazed by one small flock of sheep, and the grass is cut for hay in the

summer. Some of the Downs were ploughed during the Second World War to grow crops, but much of it has not been cultivated for centuries. The Downs are bordered at the top by the National Trust-owned Warren Woods, a patch of old, broad-leafed woodland. The Downs are bathed in wild flowers and orchids in summer and there are plenty of butterflies around. There are fine views in all directions.

THE BASICS

Distance: 3 miles (5 km)

Gradient: One gentle ascent

Severity: Easy

Approx time to walk: 1½ hours

Stiles: Two

Maps: OS Explorer 202: Leominster and Bromyard

Path description: Grass, stone tracks. The track through Warren Farm can get muddy in winter

Start Point: Public car park, next to the Royal Oak pub on the Downs road: SO670558; HR7 4QP

Parking: As above

Dog friendly: This is the ideal walk for dogs

Public Toilets: None

Nearest food: Royal Oak

BROMYARD DOWNS WALK

1. From the notice board in the car park, cross a plank bridge and climb up the Downs. There is no fixed footpath: this is common land and you can choose your own route. Bromyard Downs is one of Herefordshire's many beautiful commons and in early summer you should look out for a host of wild flowers and especially the early purple orchid. From the bridge bear half-left past a cottage on your left. Continue on the same line and head for the left-hand end of the trees on the sky-line. Cross a grass cross-path and line of trees and make for the woodland ahead, looking out for the entrance gate to Hillfield Coppice just beyond an oak tree. Enter the coppice, turn left and take a clockwise tour round the coppice back to where you came in, enjoying your first views of the Teme Valley, the Abberley Hills and, in season, the marvellous bluebells. On leaving the coppice turn left alongside the woodland and continue, maintaining your height, along a grass path through gorse and bracken. On joining a wider grass track, the Downs open up before you with Bromyard set out below. The grass track leads slightly uphill to a gate at the entrance to Shepherd's Cottage.

2. Now take this permissive route and you will soon enjoy the extensive views over the Teme Valley and, on a clear day, Worcester Cathedral. After just under a mile (1 km) you reach Warren Farm, which is a working farm, owned by the National Trust. They offer tours of the farm but you need a minimum party of 15. Continue along the main track, which bends left and starts to descend gently. Enjoy the views ahead of the Malverns and May Hill, with its 99 trees. (If you can't see May Hill in these parts, it isn't a proper walk!). After 400 metres, on a sharp left-hand bend, take a footpath to the right, walk along the side of a field, cross a stile and you are back on the Downs.

3. Now bear right, maintaining your height, admiring Bromyard set out below you, the Malverns to the south-east, May Hill to the south, the Black Mountains to the west and Titterstone Clee (with the golf ball on top) to the north. After 400 metres, go through a gate on your right into Warren Wood and enjoy this ancient mixed woodland, and, in early summer, the display of bluebells. The track goes ahead to a reservoir but we climb a stile on the left

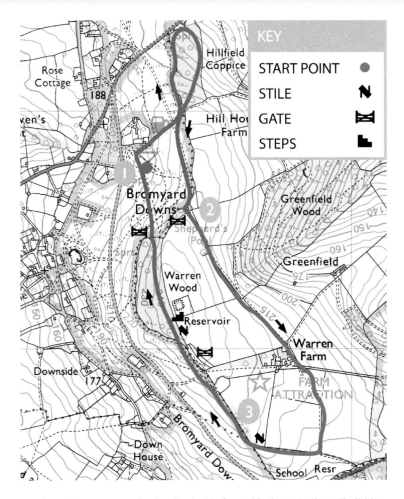

KEY

START POINT	●
STILE	N
GATE	⋈
STEPS	⌐

to continue our woodland walk. Just before a kissing gate the path divides. Take the right-hand route and climb some steps up to the side of a small reservoir. Carry on along the path until you leave the wood by a gate. Turn right along the ridge and look for a path down the hill, by any route you like, to find the car park, and its neighbour the Royal Oak, which will provide well-earned refreshment.

COLWALL

The village of Colwall nestles at the foot of the Malvern Hills, which is an Area of Outstanding Natural Beauty and once boasted a racecourse and stables.

Colwall is probably most famous as the home of Malvern Water. Malvern Water has formed a part of the national heritage and culture since Queen Elizabeth I made a point of drinking it in public in the 16th century, and Queen Victoria refused to travel without it. Malvern Water is the only bottled water used by Her Majesty, Queen Elizabeth II. It was first bottled on a commercial

scale in 1851 and sold as Malvern Soda and then as Malvern Seltzer Water from 1856. In 1890, Schweppes entered into a contract with a Colwall family, and built a bottling plant in 1892. The actual source of the spring is on the western side of the Malvern Hills in Herefordshire. The factory closed in 2010.

This walk is a gentle stroll through the surrounding pastureland and orchards, with plenty of points of interest and with the Malverns never far from our view.

Our walk passes the Winnings, which for 40 years was home to the engineer Stephen Ballard, who built the first tunnel under the Malvern Hills in 1860. When the Hereford to Worcester railway line was to be constructed

Stephen Ballard was appointed engineer for the line. The Hereford to Worcester Railway Line Act was passed in 1853 and work started in 1854. The Ledbury to Colwall section was completed in April 1861 and the tunnel through the Malverns the following year. The line was operated by the West Midland railway. One of his last works was to construct in 1884 a carriage drive along the west side of the Malvern Hills.

It was completed in October 1887 in Queen Victoria's Golden Jubilee year. Named 'Jubilee Drive' it was built on The Winnings Estate land by his employees using pick and shovel. Stephen Ballard died in December 1890 aged 86 and he and his wife and some of his family are buried in a private burial ground over the railway tunnel on The Winnings farm land.

THE BASICS

Distance: 2¾ miles (4½ km)
Gradient: Two gentle ascents
Severity: Easy
Approx time to walk: 1½ hours
Stiles: None
Maps: OS Explorer 190: Malvern Hills and Bredon Hill
Path description: Mostly pasture, orchards and firm tracks. Can be muddy after rain
Start Point: Colwall station: SO756424; WR13 6QH
Parking: Colwall station car park
Dog friendly: Yes, but dogs should be kept on a lead
Public Toilets: None
Nearest food: Colwall Coffee Lounge, The Crown Inn, Colwall Park Hotel

COLWALL WALK

1. Cross the railway bridge and follow the path past (not into) the Charlie Ballard nature reserve, which has a stream-fed pond, an amphibian pond, an alder copse and a wealth of wildlife, to a kissing gate. Walk up the left-hand side of the field and go through another kissing gate. Turn left along the hedge. At the end of the field do not go through the gate but turn right and follow the hedge up a gentle slope to the top.

Go through the gate on the left. After about 100 metres, take the left fork. As you look back, enjoy the views of the Herefordshire countryside and Hay Bluff, which is visible on a clear day. The track leads down to Hunters Lodge where it bears left, soon passing a small pond, and continues to the main road. At the road turn left and walk a short distance to Broadwood Drive. Carefully cross the road to the footpath at The Winnings. The burial ground, appropriately situated next to a tunnel shaft, is close to our route but not on the public right of way. Next to the Winnings you will see the Picton Garden and Old Court Nurseries, home to the National Michaelmas Daisy Collection and well worth a visit. Here is the birthplace of the modern asters, hybridised by Ernest Ballard (of the same family) in the early years of the twentieth century.

2. After 100 metres the path goes through a kissing gate on the left, and behind the Downs School buildings to emerge opposite the music school (ignore any paths to the right). Turn left on the track and soon right on a path between hard courts and school buildings. The path runs alongside a small orchard to a

kissing gate at Long Barn. Go straight ahead to another kissing gate. A grassy path besides school playing fields leads to a road. Turn left on the road and then right on along a footpath to a kissing gate. Enter an old orchard where the trees are laden with mistletoe. Follow the clear path eventually bearing left to the kissing gate. Follow the track to the road.

3. Turn right and then left after The Roost. Turning down this track, look up ahead to see the distinctive Herefordshire Beacon (walk 11 in this book). The track

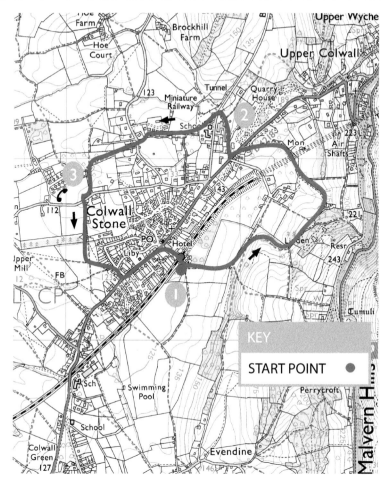

KEY

START POINT ●

leads to two kissing gates and a bridge across a stream and into a field. Follow the path up the field and bear left to the kissing gate. At the road ahead, turn right and keep straight on to the junction with the main road. Turn left. The Colwall Coffee Lounge is on the left. Further along pass the library and the children's play area and the Crown Inn. At the Colwall Park Hotel turn right to the station.

CROFT AMBREY

THIS IS AN INTERESTING WALK WITH ADDED HISTORICAL
DIMENSIONS. THE TERRAIN WHICH IT COVERS CONTRASTS
OPEN UPLAND, AFFORDING DISTANT VIEWS, WITH A LOW,
LUSH VALLEY AND ITS MORE INTIMATE ATMOSPHERE.

The walk begins at Croft Castle, which is in the care of the National Trust. It is a Welsh border castle, the stone castle superseding the earlier one of earth and timber. The Croft family has lived here for centuries with only one short break. Sir James Croft adapted the castle in 1568 to include a small brick-built mansion surrounded by formal terraced gardens. The house is well worth a visit, as is the delightful little church nearby with its early Croft tombs.

The route climbs steadily up to Croft Ambrey, the midway destination of this walk. These earthworks are nearly a thousand feet (300 metres) above sea level and are an excellent example of an Iron Age hill-fort, being a large multi-enclosure site dating from Celtic times. It was built in a hugely strategic position and modern visitors too can appreciate the far-reaching views over the countryside.

The steep-sided and heavily wooded Fishpool Valley is criss-crossed with intriguing paths. Our return route takes us alongside all five pools before rising back up to the level of the parkland. This very special valley, like much of this walk, is owned by the National Trust. Various walks have been laid out and marked by coloured arrows. We follow parts of them.

THE WALK

1.   Walk to the top of the car park. Having passed through the visitor reception bear right along a path and through the kissing gate next to a cattle grid. Keep to the metal road and follow the red and blue arrow way mark signs. Go right round a bend gradually going uphill. The road soon turns into a track and immediately before a large gate turn left through a pedestrian gate still following red and blue way mark signs. Continue on this track for 100 metres to the next gate that takes you into an open field. Follow the marker posts uphill. You will soon notice you are following a renowned avenue of old sweet (Spanish) chestnut trees. Many of these are in a poor state and happily there is significant replacement taking place. Climb steadily towards Croft Wood but before entering, pause at the rustic seats and take time to look at the near 180o distant views, particularly to the Black Mountains in the south-west.

THE BASICS

Distance: 3 miles (4½ km)

Gradient: One gradual slope upwards, then the equivalent down

Severity: Moderate

Approx time to walk: 1¾ hours

Stiles: None

Map: OS Explorer 203: Ludlow

Path description: Mostly tarmac or firm tracks but the downhill section is likely to be muddy

Start point: 5 miles (8 km) north-west of Leominster, 9 miles (15 km) south-west of Ludlow: SO455655; HR6 9PW

Parking: National Trust car park (fee usually applicable, unless the car owner is a NT member but it allows one into the castle grounds as well)

Dog friendly: Yes

Public Toilets: At the Croft Castle tea rooms, adjacent to the car park

Nearest food: National Trust cafe adjacent to the car park

2. Go through the kissing gate and continue uphill following the path sign posted "Footpath to Croft Ambrey." Where a broad track crosses, keep straight on. Croft Wood is mainly conifer though there are plans to restore more broad leaf species. Evidence has been found of charcoal burning here in the old days. On approaching the next gate follow the blue arrow to the right going through a small gate. Keep on this path, continuing to follow the blue arrow left then left again. You are now on the path at the base of the hill-fort walking in a clockwise direction. The path eventually curves round to the right to a cleft in the earthen ramparts. This was once the south-west entrance to the fort. When it was excavated in the 1960's, evidence of a heavily fortified entrance with timber gates and a guard room was revealed. As you proceed the vistas open out. Notice the steep bank and ditch over to your right, constructed for defensive purposes, though the ramparts are much reduced from their earlier size. At the highest point, pause to look at the stunning views-Clee Hills to the north-east and the Welsh hills to the west. In the foreground is the quarry at Leinthall Earls, a reminder of present day endeavours. Continue along this high level path and then follow the clear track down to what was the east gate. Shortly a blue arrow sign will be seen, indicating a route going off to the right. Ignore this unless you seek a shorter way back. Instead, continue on downhill, passing an ancient yew tree. Soon after go through a gate and then turn right. After a short distance look out for a footpath turning off on your right. This is marked by the green Mortimer Trail logo). Also at this same point is a distinctive tree. This is one of many hornbeams that once ringed the fort. Go through this gate.

3. The next section of the route leads down to the Fishpool Valley. This set of five pools where once fish were kept for the castle inhabitants to eat, is a site of Special Scientific Interest because of the ferns, flowers, birds, mosses, liverwort and rare crayfish that flourish in these particular damp surroundings. Ash (where it has survived) and also oak, beech, yew, and wychelm have been recorded. The pools are quiet now. In fact it is a mysterious, damp area that contrasts with the brightness of the hill-fort just visited.

Follow the footpath downhill. Take care as it is invariably muddy. On reaching a T-junction of paths, cross over to another even smaller footpath. As the path descends and becomes narrower, mud and stones can make it quite slippery. Again continue downwards until another T-junction is reached. These tracks which cross our route were laid out in 1780

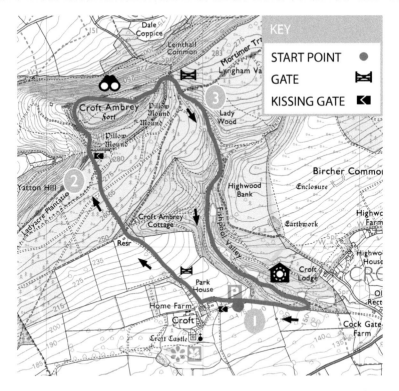

in a period of extensive landscaping to provide carriage rides for the castle folk. Continue over to the next small downhill path, and on meeting yet another of these tracks, this time join it, heading right. A small brick building housing a pumping engine on your right will indicate you are near the first of the fish pools. This will be seen on your left. The state of the water will vary according to the time of year. A 'land bridge' separates the first from the second pool. On your right at this point you will pass an old limekiln set into an old quarry smothered in ferns. This is one of two in the valley and was first recorded in 1890. Continue on the downward path, still enjoying the valley route which passes all the pools. Between pools 3 and 4 is a gothic pumphouse, used originally to pump up spring water to the castle. At the next fork, keep left. You are now on the yellow arrow route. These last pools are spring fed and look different to the others. At the next fork, go left as indicated by the yellow arrow. After passing the final pool take the right fork which will lead you gradually up from the valley bottom and out onto the park. At the park drive, turn right and soon the car park will be visible. At the end of your walk, stop for tea in the castle's 'Carpenters's Cafe'. Toilets and shops are also situated here.

EWYAS HARALD - DORE ABBEY

Ewyas Harald is an interesting, friendly village, far more self-sufficient than many Herefordshire villages, boasting a church, school, fire station, doctors' surgery, two pubs, a tea room, fish and chip restaurant, and a village store.

Ewyas means 'sheep area' and Harald acquired the castle at the time of the Domesday Book. It was his son who founded Dore Abbey. Dore Abbey, our destination on this walk, is in the Golden Valley, a name based on a linguistic confusion between the Welsh word dwr meaning water and the French words d'or meaning golden. The valley was originally noted for its water because of the extensive irrigation carried out along the valley in the 16th century. The walk crosses Ewyas Harald common en route to Dore Abbey. We return via a different route across the common.

Ewyas Harold Common covers an area of 126 acres on a plateau above Herefordshire's Golden Valley, and rises to 164m (538 feet) at its highest point. From the top of the common there are wonderful views of Garway and Saddlebow hills to the east, the Skirrid to the south, and the Black Mountains and Hay Bluff to the west. The common is a magnificent wild space and an important local amenity. It contains numerous relics of past use, including quarries, lime kilns, orchards and abandoned house sites. And it is a wildlife oasis, rich in butterflies, flowers and fungi, and an excellent site for bird watching.

The Cistercian Abbey of Dore was founded in 1147. After the Dissolution of the Monasteries in 1535, the Abbey fell into ruin and at one time was used to house cattle. However, in 1632 John, Viscount Scudamore was persuaded by Bishop Laud to restore the abbey in the hope that God would answer his prayers for a male heir. The abbey was re-consecrated in 1634. And, praise be, Scudamore's wife duly produced a son. The abbey has remained a regular place of worship.

THE BASICS

Distance: 3½ miles (5½ km)

Gradient: One short steep climb, one gentle climb

Severity: Moderate

Approx time to walk: 1½ hours

Stiles: Two

Map: OS Outdoor Leisure 13: Brecon Beacons (eastern area)

Path description: Mainly grassland and tracks which can be muddy, especially in winter

Start Point: Ewyas Harald village centre: SO387286; HR2 0EX

Parking: Street parking in the village

Dog Friendly: Yes, but dogs on leads in the bird nesting season and near sheep or ponies. Both pubs in Ewyas Harald are dog friendly

Public Toilets: Dore Abbey

Nearest food: The Dog; The Temple Bar; Stables fish and chips; Abbey Dore Court tearoom; Neville Arms, Abbey Dore

1. Walk up School Lane between the two pubs. Walk past the school and turn left. As the road winds round up the hill, you reach a cattle grid at the entrance to Ewyas Harald Common, complete with information board. Enjoy the fine views into Wales on your left. Continue up the hill on the main track and when the track divides take the right fork on a stone and mud track continuing uphill.

2. When you meet a stone cross-track, turn sharp right, enjoying the tree-lined route and after 200 metres you join a further track coming in from the left to emerge at a junction of tracks. Turn sharp left past a second information board and Newholme. After 100 metres, bear left, maintaining your height, onto open grassland. Now follow the path on the right-hand edge of the common. Continue to follow the path through woodland on the right-hand edge, admiring the views of Saddlebow and Garway hills to your right, to Cider Barn. Carry on down the main track past Cider Barn, leave the common, and reach the road to Abbey Dore. Turn left along the road for 500 metres, passing the Neville Arms. Look out for the sign to Dore Abbey.

3. After visiting the abbey, return to the road, cross it, go over a stile and go straight up the hill to a rather difficult steep stile. Carry on straight up the steep bank. At the top of the bank you will find a magnificent oak tree. Pause here to wonder at the unexpected sight of a London tube train on the other side of the Golden Valley (an SAS training facility). Now turn left with the hedge on your right to a metal gate by a house, The Green. This brings you back out onto an open part of the common where ponies often graze. Turn left past The Green. Keep to the left-hand side of the common with the hedge on your left to reach New House, clad in wood shingles. Turn right across the grass gallops with Garway Hill and its mast ahead of you.

After 300 metres, bear half-right, staying on the main broad gallop. Pass a small mound with some newly planted trees on your right. Here you will find a bench and the 'lonesome pine' in memory of Nancy Hall. This is a good place to enjoy a picnic. Resuming our walk, bear half-right, still on a wide grass track, with gorse on your right. After a short distance, look out for and go towards the chimney pots of a house tucked in below the bank. When you reach the stone

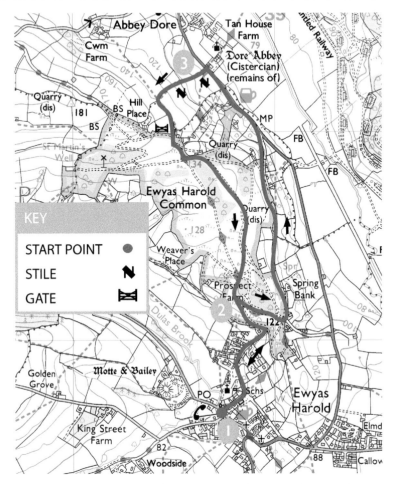

KEY

START POINT ●

STILE ✦

GATE ⬄

track and the house, turn left, go past the bench on your left and you will soon be back at pont (2). Retrace your path to the village.

HAUGH WOOD

HAUGH WOOD LIES SOUTHEAST OF HEREFORD WITHIN THE
PARISHES OF FOWNHOPE, WOOLHOPE AND MORDIFORD. IT
IS ONE OF THE MOST IMPORTANT WOODLAND SITES FOR
NATURE CONSERVATION IN THE REGION

And is nationally important for the 600-plus species of butterflies and moths found within its boundaries. In order for everyone to enjoy the butterflies, Forest Enterprise and Butterfly Conservation have set up two marked trails through the woods. This walk follows these trails and provides an excellent introduction to this beautiful area.

The name Haugh is an ancient name of Saxon origin and these woods have a long and fascinating history. At the time of Domesday, Fownhope Manor was one of the wealthiest in the county and Woolhope Manor was owned by the Canons of Hereford cathedral. Haugh Wood is not actually mentioned by name but an area of wood and wasteland is recorded. The earliest reference to Haugh Wood by name is in 1544 when the Crown valued part of the wood around Fownhope. Again in 1601, the year of Queen Elizabeth I's death, the name Haugh Wood is recorded when it was leased to Sir John Scudamore. From this time on there are many records outlining the careful management of the woods for coppicing and charcoal burning by its various owners.

The 1840s tithe surveys and maps for Fownhope, Mordiford and Woolhope delineate almost exactly the boundaries and area of the present-day wood. The wood provided an excellent habitat for game and the richness of its wildlife was also recorded by the Victorian naturalists of the time. Then in 1925 the Forestry Commission started to purchase parts of the wood. The ancient natural trees were felled and the woods re-planted with larch, beech, douglas fir and oak as part of a national policy to build up the stock of home-grown timber.

However, in 1995 there was a complete change of policy. The UK Biodiversity Action Plan included the concept of restoring selected ancient woodland sites and converting them back to a semi-natural condition, and this included Haugh Wood. Some years later in 2006 the Forestry Commission committed itself to the complete restoration of this woodland to a traditionally worked semi-natural woodland by 2040. Forest Enterprise, which is part of the Commission, is now undertaking this challenging task of restoration. Now let's set off to explore their work and enjoy our heritage!

THE BASICS

Distance: 3½ or 1½ miles (5½ or 2½ km)

Gradient: Undulating with some short steeper sections

Severity: Moderate

Approx time to walk: 2 (1) hours

Stiles: None

Map: OS Explorer 189: Hereford and Ross-on-Wye

Path description: Maintained forestry paths and woodland footpaths with some muddy sections

Car Park and Start Point: On the road half way between Mordiford and Woolhope From Mordiford the car park is 1¼ m on the left before post code HR1 4QX

Grid Ref for car park SO592365

Dog friendly: Yes

Public Toilets: None

Nearest food: Pubs in Mordiford, Woolhope and Fownhope

HAUGH WOOD WALK

1. Start the walk from the far left-hand side of the car park. Here is an information board, a barrier to stop vehicles entering the woods, and the first of the 'red' butterfly trail signs. This trail forms the first part of the walk and is 1½ miles (2½ km) long. Walk straight ahead and read about the butterflies that you may see in the wood during the summer months. Take note of the trees, many of which  are now native deciduous trees, and the numerous wild flowers that have been encouraged to grow by cutting back the edges of the woodland.

2. Turn left at the next red arrow. Look back to see the "dragon" feeding boxes on the tree. There is local legend about a dragon that lived in the woods above Mordiford. A little girl called Maud brought it food and the local children have made the boxes as part of a project to remember the story and bring it to life. Now go on following the red arrows. After turning right again, go down until you reach a gateway on the left just past a wooden seat. Through the gateway is a noticeboard giving information about Joanshill Farm which is not far away. This nature reserve is a microcosm of the old Herefordshire landscape of hay meadows and orchards enclosed by thick hedgerows and has wonderful wild flowers in early summer.

3. Don't go through the gateway but follow the bridleway round to the right.

4. Watch out for a sharp turn right up a smaller track to climb uphill through the woods. This track, which can be muddy, flattens out and leads back to the car park. At quiet times you may hear rustling and see some of the fallow deer that live in these wonderful woods.

5. After a refreshment stop at the picnic tables, cross the road and go round the barrier to follow the "green" butterfly trail signs. This trail makes up the second part of this walk and is about two miles long. It is quieter on this side of the wood so once again look and listen out for the deer and read the information about the butterflies. The green arrows guide you round to the left and then right at a T-junction.

6. The path continues down through the wood before reaching a pleasant little valley of green pastureland to your left.

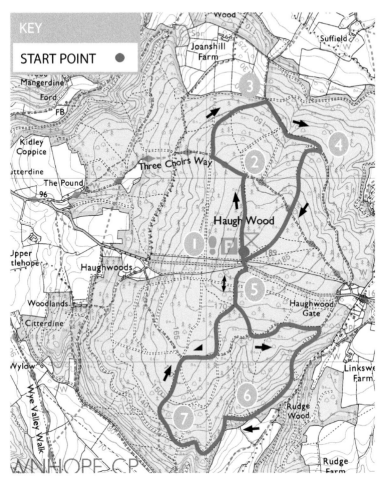

KEY

START POINT ●

7.   At another junction with a steep path coming up on the left, you turn right steeply uphill to find a seat on the left where you can rest and enjoy the view. Then go

about 10 metres past the seat and turn up a narrow track to the right clearly signed by the green arrow and follow it upwards until you reach a wide path. Turn left here and shortly afterwards you pass a wooden seat. Take the track just beyond it and shortly afterwards turn right along another twisty track through the pine woods. When you reach the main path turn left and follow it back to the car park.

HAYWOOD PARK & BELMONT

THE WALK LIES TO THE SOUTH WEST OF THE CENTRE OF HEREFORD. IT COVERS WOODLAND, OPEN GRASS LAND AND THE NEW HAYWOOD PARK, WHICH IS STILL BEING DEVELOPED.

Here you will find some sculptures and a playground for small children. Feeding the ducks is also popular. Midway around you will cross the grounds of Belmont Abbey with an opportunity to have a close look, and also to stop at Hedley Lodge for refreshments. The final section of the walk takes you across fields with excellent views of the city. Finally you return to the built-up area, passing in front of Tesco (always useful for a little shopping, refreshments and toilets).

THE WALK

1.   From the car park return to the road, turn right, and walk along the grassy verge past some trees to a public footpath sign. Turn right and walk along the edge of the playing field. Go through a gate at the top of the field into woodland and follow the path bearing left. At a junction of paths turn left and walk a short distance to a bench, turn right along a narrow grassy track and follow it down and to the right, and continue through another wood and onward to a large track. Turn left, go through the gate into Haywood Park, then turn immediately left on a grassy track; follow this around the field climbing up towards a house. At the junction of paths go right, and take a short detour to your right to the viewpoint. Retrace your steps, and follow the path over the top of the parkland dropping down to a track surrounding the lovely Belmont Pool.

2.   Turn right to walk alongside the pool with a good opportunity for a picnic; there is also a playground to the right of the bridge you will cross to continue around the lake. Here there is easy access to feed the ducks. Continue along the path to join a residential road, turn left along the grassy verge above the lake to a small

THE BASICS

Distance: 4 miles (6½ km)
Gradient: Slight
Severity: Easy
Approx time to walk: 2 hours
Stiles: Two
Map: OS Explorer 189: Hereford and Ross-on-Wye
Path Description: Grass paths and metalled tracks or roads
Start Point: Southolme Road car park, Hereford (off A465 Tesco roundabout): SO494379; HR2 7TZ
Parking: As above
Dog Friendly: Yes
Public Toilets: None on route, nearest at Tesco
Nearest food: Hedley Lodge

path leading to Haywood Lane and turn right, taking great care crossing this road to the opposite pavement. Walk up to the main road and continue along the pavement for a short distance to a gate on your left leading into Belmont Woods. Enter the wood and look at the beautiful yew tree on your left, then take the lower path down towards the pool, which is not accessible. Follow the track as it winds its way through the wood (there is one handy place to reach the stream opposite a bench). When the track rises and meets another, turn left and continue, avoiding any small paths on your left, until reaching a junction in sight of the road. Go left to the road and leave the woods. Carefully cross the busy A465,

turn right to walk to the entrance of Belmont Abbey, turn in and walk along the central road passing the Parish Church of Belmont on your left, and then further along Hedley Lodge, where you will be able to have refreshments, and the Abbey, tucked slightly behind and off this road. Founded in 1859, Belmont Abbey is a monastery of the English Benedictine Congregation dedicated to St Michael and All Angels. Since its foundation Belmont has served as a cathedral and a monastic house of studies. It has played an important part in the development of monasticism in Great Britain.

3.   Turn left towards the Abbey and, if you have time, look around it, then turn right on yourself to walk through a wooden gate. Cross the road to a stile in front of you and continue straight down the field, enjoying the magnificent views of the cathedral, water tower and spires of Hereford on your far right. Turn right at the

bottom and walk towards a second stile; cross this and continue along the path to a road. Cross to continue along a footpath. At the next road cross it, bearing slightly right, to walk in the same direction alongside a stream. Pass a bridge on your left and

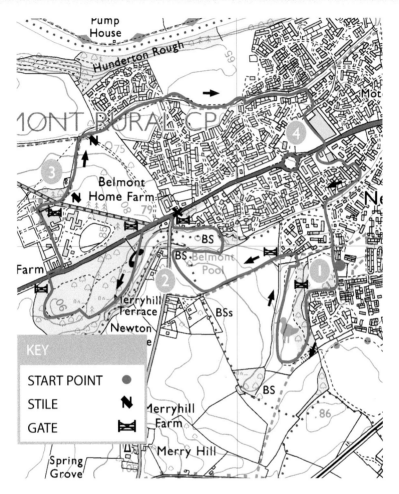

houses on your right. Just before a second bridge you will see a path, usually with a bin marking the spot, on your right leading towards a road. Follow this to the back of Tesco, turn right, and cross the pedestrian crossing to walk along the frontage of Tesco and a small section of car park, climb up to the A456 and another pedestrian crossing, cross and turn right.

4.   Walk around the Belmont Community Centre, and continue around the pharmacy, joining another path. Go right then left on a road towards Eastholme Avenue, follow this path to a broad grassy area then a grassy track to Southolme Road by a mini roundabout. Walk left up the road back to the car park.

HEREFORDSHIRE BEACON

This walk features the southern end of the Malvern Hills. It is an undulating walk through the Malvern Hills conservators' and Eastnor estate lands, which are designated as an Area of Outstanding Natural Beauty.

The Malvern Hills have been described as a mountain range in miniature; the eight mile ridge contains some of the oldest rocks in Britain and their craggy outline is reminiscent of the uplands further west into Wales. A walk in the hills is strenuous enough that Mallory walked here in preparation for his ascent of Everest. Today you can enjoy over 3000 acres of open countryside climbing to the highest point at Worcestershire Beacon or relax whilst quietly rambling along the wooded slopes. Edward Elgar was born in the shadow of the Malverns and these hills were a source of inspiration for his music. Indeed his cantata Caractacus (1898) is set on British Camp, the iron age hill-fort which we visit on our walk. In 1934, during the composer's final illness, he told a friend: "If ever after I'm dead you hear someone whistling this tune [the opening theme of his cello concerto] on the Malvern Hills, don't be alarmed. It's only me."

There are extensive views over the surrounding counties and the walk contains many interesting geological features, but the highlight is undoubtedly the Iron Age fort of British Camp.

At the start we walk along the ridge of the Malvern Hills. We then go down into a woodland area, followed by the extensive Eastnor estate. After a short climb up to the obelisk, the route drops down to the estate's lakes. Another short climb and the wooded limestone ridgeway is reached before we make our final ascent to the top of Herefordshire Beacon, at 338 metres above sea level

THE WALK

1. Leave the car park through the gate to the right-hand side, next to the information board. The path climbs to a level track which we follow. Ignore uphill paths to the right. In a short distance look out for a reservoir on the left-hand side, with the Severn plain in the distance, and to the right a spectacular view of the defensive ramparts of the Iron Age British Camp. Continue along this path until you reach a stone direction indicator. Follow the path for Clutters Cave. The cave is said to have been occupied by a hermit. Immediately beyond the cave, take the left-hand path. This will take you to Hangman's Hill where public hangings, often for very minor offences, took place.

THE BASICS

Distance: 5 miles (8 km)

Gradient: Several short climbs

Severity: Moderate

Approx time to walk: 3 hours

Stiles: None

Map: OS Explorer 190: Malvern Hills and Bredon Hill

Start Point: British Camp car park: SO764404; WR13 6DW

Path: Mainly well-maintained tracks and paths, firm under foot

Parking: Pay and display car park

Dog friendly: Yes, but on leads near animals. One cattle grid could be tricky for some dogs

Public Toilets: Opposite the car park

Nearest food: British Camp hotel; refreshment hut in the car park

From this viewpoint you will see that this area is out of line with the rest of the more northern hills. This was caused by tremendous earth pressures which pushed Herefordshire Beacon nearly half a mile (almost a kilometre) west of the main axis of the hills. Also at this point there is a very good illustration of the shire ditch which runs along the ridge of the hills. This was

constructed around 1290 to define the boundaries between the Bishop of Hereford's land and that of Gilbert de Clare, the owner of the land to the east of the hills.

Continue southwards, enjoying the exhilarating ridge walk. At the end of the ridge, take the steep path down to a junction of five paths. Take the second path on the right, signed to the Gullet and Midsummer Hill. Go up the hill and follow the ridge until a stone marker is reached on the right-hand side. Follow the path on the right, signed to the obelisk, which descends steeply down the hill.

2. Go through the metal gate or cattle grid at the bottom left-hand corner and proceed down the wide track through the woodland. At the bottom of a slope, straight ahead, can be seen the other Iron Age fort of Midsummer Hill. Perhaps visit this site on a subsequent visit to the area. Go through two gates on the right-hand side and into the Eastnor deer park. Go straight ahead up the hill until you

reach the obelisk on the left-hand side of the track. The obelisk was built in 1812 in memory of Edward Somers, whose family owned the castle and estate at Eastnor. It was designed by Robert Smirke, architect of the British Museum.

3. Follow the main metalled track straight ahead and down the hill through open parkland, looking out for views of Eastnor Castle on the left, and admiring the hollowed tree on your route. The massive castle, built in Norman Revival style, was completed in 1820. It is well worth visiting but do check opening times. At a T-junction turn right and then left to cross a small bridge across the lakes. Take the tarmac road up the hill. At the top turn right behind the lodge along a private road (walkers are permitted to use it) and along the wooded ridgeway for about 1½ miles (2½ km) until you reach the A449.

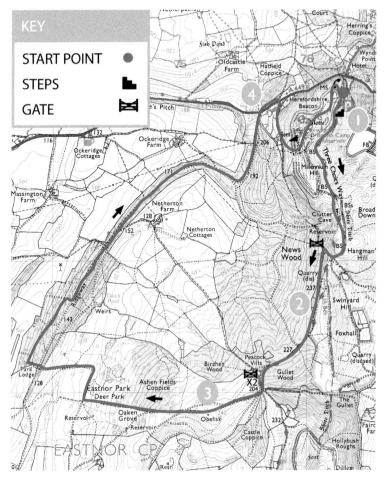

KEY

START POINT ●

STEPS ▟

GATE ✕

4. Turn right and with very great care walk along the verge of this road for 150 metres. Turn right into a wide track just beyond Beacon Lodge. Follow this track until you reach a path on the left-hand side. This is 50 metres before a stile. If you reach the

stile you have gone too far. Climb up this steep path to the first of the British Camp defensive ramparts. Cross over the ditch and walk up the hill onto the top of the Iron Age fort of British Camp. The ditch and bank around the site in fact covers three hills, although those to north and south are little more than spurs. With a perimeter of 6,800 feet (2,070 metres) the defences enclose an area of around 44 acres. The first earthworks were around the base of the central hill but at least four prehistoric phases of building have so far been identified. There is no evidence about whether the coming of the Romans ended the use of the British Camp, but folklore states that the ancient British chieftain Caratacus made his last stand here. This is unlikely, according to the description of the Roman historian Tacitus, who implies a site closer to the River Severn. Excavations at Midsummer Hill-fort, Bredon Hill and Croft Ambrey all show evidence of violent destruction around AD 48, three years before the capture of Caratacus. This may suggest that the British Camp was abandoned or destroyed around the same time.

Now you are on top of Herefordshire Beacon and you can enjoy unparalleled views in all directions: Black Mountains to the west, Worcestershire Beacon and beyond to Clee Hill to the north, Bredon Hill and the Severn Vale to the east and May Hill to the south.

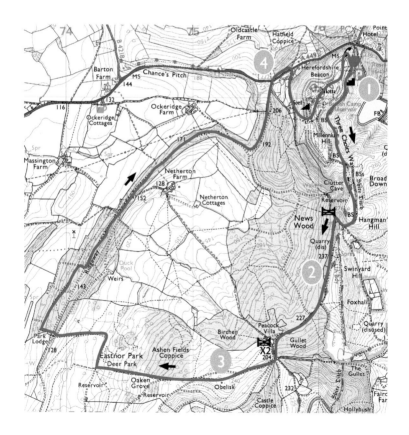

The diarist John Evelyn (1620–1706) remarked that the view from the hill was 'one of the godliest vistas in England'. It is then but a short walk back down to the car park where welcome refreshments may be obtained.

HERGEST RIDGE, KINGTON

KINGTON IS ONE OF THE GREAT SMALL TOWNS OF BRITAIN:
AN ELEGANT MEDIEVAL MARKET TOWN, STILL IN EVERYDAY USE
BY SOME OF THE DESCENDANTS OF THE PEOPLE WHO BUILT IT.

The Kington hinterland was once one of the country's largest Neolithic settlements, and is studded with Bronze Age tombs, medieval motte and bailey castles and ancient churches. Kington is situated close to the Welsh border and for centuries was a centre for cattle drovers. Present-day walkers are spoilt for choice. The Offa's Dyke Path, the Arrow Valley trail and and the Herefordshire Trail run through Kington and the 30-mile (50 km) Mortimer's Trail from Ludlow finishes at Kington. In addition a web of footpaths, accessible on foot from the town centre, is waiting for you. Kington is a 'Walkers are Welcome' town, and even boasts its own walking festival in September. Details are available on the website at www.kingtonwalks.org.

Rising above the town is Hergest Ridge, the setting for our lovely walk, which covers a section of the Offa's Dyke long-distance path along the English/Welsh border. Look out for mountain ponies and red kite. The long but gentle climb up this broad ridge offers stunning views over Herefordshire to the south and Powys to the north. On your way to the start you will pass Hergest Croft Gardens, which are well worth visiting after your walk. There are gorgeous flower borders, an old-fashioned kitchen garden, an azalea garden, maple grove, and extensive woodland. And there's the lure of a cream tea at the end.

THE WALK

1. Walk up the last bit of road and through a metal gate on to the open hillside. You are now walking along Offa's Dyke path. Offa's Dyke Path is one of twelve designated National Trails. It is the only national trail to follow a man-made feature. Built by Offa, King of Mercia between AD 757 and 796, the dyke formed the boundary between England and Wales, running 182 miles (293 km) from Prestatyn in the north to Sedbury, near Chepstow in the south. A broad path leads you gently uphill. At the first fingerpost keep straight ahead.

THE BASICS

Distance: 4½ miles (7½ km)

Gradient: Gentle

Severity: Easy when taken slowly

Approx time to walk: 2 hours

Stiles: None

Map: OS Explorer 201: Knighton and Presteigne

Start Point: Kington: SO281567; HR5 3EG

Path: Soft springy turf over open hillside

Parking: At the top of the No Through Road close to the 'Thank you for visiting Kington' sign

Dog friendly: Yes, but dogs on leads near sheep

Public Toilets: None

Nearest food: Tea at Hergest Croft Gardens when open. Otherwise the pubs, cafes and restaurants of Kington

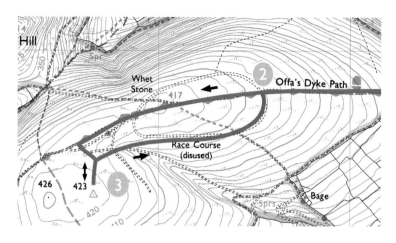

2. At the second marker post take the right-hand path of three and up to a welcome bench where you can enjoy the superb views opening up to your right of Bradnor Hill and Rushock Hill. Continue ahead, ignoring the signpost over to the left. As the path levels out, you approach signposts on left and right, and you will see a large anvil-shaped rock on the left which is known as the whetstone. This is probably an outlier from the ice age but legend suggests it was an old meeting/trading place. Keep straight ahead, enjoying the views of the Black Mountains and Brecon Beacons and at the next signpost still go straight ahead to reach a small pond. Here turn left and walk to the trig point to marvel at the 360-degree views with the Malvern Hills, the Pyons, Burton Hill and Ivington hill-fort now visible to the east.

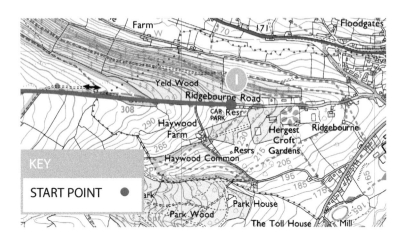

KEY

START POINT ●

3. Retrace your steps to the pond and turn sharp right. This path crosses the head of the dingle towards the monkey puzzle trees (planted by the owner

of Hergest Gardens). However, well before the trees your path meets a broad track which was once an old racecourse. Take this to the right. Keep left at a fork and before long you will come back to the second marker post at (2). Go right, retracing your steps to the start.

KINGSTHORNE, ACONBURY & LTTLE BIRCH

A WALK THROUGH TIME – THIS LONGER WALK EXPLORES SOME OF THE HISTORY AROUND THESE VILLAGES. KINGSTHORNE AND LITTLE BIRCH ARE PLEASANT VILLAGES SOUTH OF HEREFORD JUST EAST OF THE BUSY A49.

They have a mixture of new and old dwellings and many historical features which are interesting windows on a past way of life.

The woodland on Aconbury Hill was once much more extensive. It was a protected royal forest, the first historical record being in 1213 when King John licensed William Cantilupe to take 33 oaks to fortify Hereford Castle. In 1216 he allowed a small area of forest to become farmland to support the nuns at Aconbury Priory. By the 1700s the estates had been sold to the Governors of Guy's Hospital in London who extensively felled the timber, sending much of it to the King's Dockyards. By the late 1700s much of the summit had become open farmland, but this was reforested by the late 1800s and remains today as a managed woodland.

Aconbury Priory was fairly extensive but all that remains now is the little church which was restored in the 1800s but is now closed. Near to the church are springs which feed the pools by the lane. In the past these acted as fishponds for the Priory. Up in the field on the right the spring is known as St Ann's Well. This was believed to have medicinal properties, with the first bucketful of water collected on Twelfth Night being the best and said to cure eye troubles. In the field on the left is another holy spring haunted by the spirits of two lovers and called Ladywell. Obviously these wells have been used by settlers since ancient times and the folklore relating to them is fascinating.

On the other side of the woods in Little Birch is a much larger well named Higgins Well. Legend relates that a well higher up the hill was filled in by a Mr Higgins who was annoyed that villagers trespassed on his land to obtain water. Soon after this unfriendly act, his living room was flooded by a new spring and to appease the spirits he quickly re-opened the well but at its present site. The current stonework was erected in the 1900s, so that the well now has two levels, one for domestic use and the other for animals. The water is very pure and flows constantly.

A more recent episode in history is commemorated by the Violette Szabo GC Museum in Wormelow and the Trail of the same name which you encounter on this walk. The trail was launched by the Allied Special Forces Association in the year 2000. It follows six miles (10 km) of footpaths and lanes from the outskirts of Hereford to the Museum, which is well worth a visit. Both the Trail and the Museum celebrate the life of Violette Szabo, who was born in 1921 and later worked for the Special Operations Executive as part of the Resistance in France during the Second World War. In 1944 she was captured and shot by the Gestapo. She frequently stayed with her cousins in Wormelow and the present owner of the house has set up the museum as a tribute to her bravery.

THE BASICS

Distance: 6 miles (10 km)
Gradient: Some short steep ascents and descents
Severity: Moderate
Approx time to walk: 3 hours
Stiles: Five
Maps: OS Explorer 189: Hereford and Ross-on-Wye
Path description: Woodland, field paths and lanes – some uneven or muddy
Start Point: Kingsthorne bus stop and car park: SO 498321; HR2 8AL
Parking: Small free car park at start
Dog friendly: Keep dogs on leads near livestock and on lanes
Public Toilets: none
Nearest food: Axe and Cleaver, Much Birch; Grafton Hotel, Hereford

1. Start the walk from the car park by the bus stop in Kingsthorne. Go back towards Hereford for about 50 metres and turn up a track on the right that leads past some dwellings to the edge of the woods. Carry straight on through a metal gate at the footpath signs and then after about 100 metres bear right onto a marked footpath (yellow arrow) up through the woodland, bearing left at the next yellow arrow to reach a crossroads of footpaths. To left and right is the ditch and straight ahead

   is the rampart of Aconbury Iron Age hill-fort which dates from 800 BC. Walk up through the gap in the ramparts and onto the inner more level area. At the top turn left and shortly after take the marked footpath to the right that winds steeply down, crossing two forest tracks and then reaching a wide path. Go straight across and follow the track right down to a stile. (In places you can see through the trees what a good vantage point these ancient Iron Age people had from their lofty home. Take the path across the field to the lane and turn right.

2. Follow the lane round to the little hamlet of Aconbury. Here you can see where the nuns established their Augustine Priory in the 1300s and admire the little church which marks the spot. Retrace your steps back from the church and take the second marked path to the left just past the small pond (St Ann's Well). Bearing slightly left and then right follow the short stream heading back up towards the woods. Continue into the woods along quite a steep track and on reaching the wide forest track turn right and then left to follow the footpath up through the woods. Watch out for a turn off to the right at the footpath sign (yellow arrow). Cross two stiles then walk up along the field edge with the woods on your right followed by another stile towards the top. At a junction of paths, take the left-hand turn down a track bearing the sign 'Violette Szabo GC Trail'. Follow the track and cross the lane to take one of the many Green Lanes and Byways that are a feature of Kingsthorne and Little Birch. After a while this becomes a paved lane which later bears right and then left to go downhill.

3. Take the next turn left (marked by a 'No through road' sign) and follow the lane up and round to the right and walk down between the houses and hedges to discover Higgins Well. From the well, take the track lane to the right along to Little Birch Church. This small church has been rebuilt in the Victorian style of the 1800s but still has a Norman font and stunning intricate ironwork.

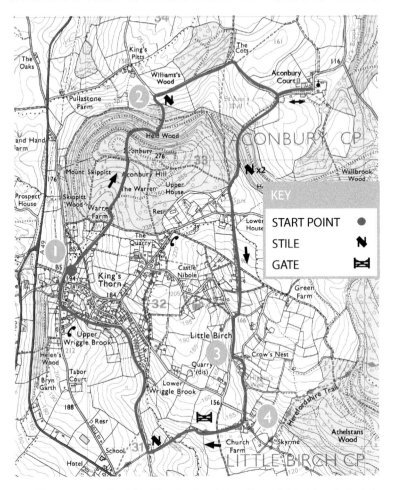

4. Take the lane to the right of the church and almost immediately take a footpath to the right through the fields by the farm. Turn right through the gate. You will notice from the signs that we have now joined the Herefordshire Trail. This is a circular walk of some 154 miles (250 km) and was devised by the Hereford Group of the Ramblers Association to link up the market towns by a beautiful scenic route all round the county. The path crosses the hedgerow and continues straight across along a green lane. At the end go through a gate and at the second line of trees on your left turn down the field bearing away from the trees to cross a bridge over the Wriggle Brook. The path on the other side goes uphill to a new gate, over a stile, and then up along the hedge to the lane. Turn right along the lane and take the first turn left to follow the brook steeply up the valley. Take the left fork again and follow it right up to the main road, turn right and, taking care, walk past the houses to the bus stop and car park.

LEDBURY

NAMED IN THE DOMESDAY BOOK AS LIEDEBERGE, LEDBURY
IS A BUSTLING MARKET TOWN WITH A POPULATION OF
9,600.

Although the livestock market closed in 1999, the town is still a busy service centre for the surrounding villages and hamlets, characterised by a range of independent shops – which will make a pleasant diversion halfway around the walk.

To the east of Ledbury rise the Malvern Hills, an eight-mile (13 km) ridge of some of the oldest rocks in Britain rising to nearly 1400 feet (425 metres) above the Severn plain. Ledbury is surrounded by rich agricultural land, mainly used for pasture, orchards and soft fruits. In recent years the town has become known for its annual poetry festival which takes place in early July and builds on the association of Ledbury with poets such as William Langland, the 14th-century creator of Piers Plowman, and Elizabeth Barrett Browning, who spent her childhood at Hope End, just outside the town. John Masefield, poet laureate from 1930 to 1967, was born in Ledbury. The town is characterised by many historical black-and-white buildings including the 17th-century Market House.

This short walk encompasses a variety of terrain and scenery. At the start we walk uphill thorough an orchard to a mixed deciduous wood. Then we follow a broad, level track along an old green lane before descending to the historic town centre where there are ample opportunities for rest and refreshment or a spot of retail therapy. From the town centre, the walk continues, firstly via a short stretch through a built-up area, and then along a disused railway track which runs along the edge of the recreation ground and then through attractive trees until you are back at the start point.

For children the recreation ground contains a wide range of play equipment and there are also some adult exercise facilities for anyone who needs to burn up a few of the extra calories consumed in the cafes earlier.

THE WALK

1.   From the station, turn right and pass under the railway bridge. On the right, about 50 metres from the bridge, there is a stile on the right which leads to a footpath through an orchard. Do not fear; this is the only stile on the route. Follow this well-trodden path uphill with the hedge on your right and the orchard on your left. Eventually this uphill path meets another. Turn diagonally right to go through a metal kissing gate. Turn right onto a metalled track and proceed to a road. This metalled track goes across the portal to Ledbury Tunnel and you can look down onto the railway tracks and marvel at how far you've climbed. Cross the road, watching the traffic. Go up about six steps into Dog Hill Wood and immediately turn left. Follow an undulating, rather rough path for about 500 metres which runs along the edge of the wood above the road. The path swings to the right into the wood and soon meets the broad green lane, an ancient packhorse route to Worcester.

THE BASICS

Distance: 2 miles (3 km)

Gradient: One short climb

Severity: Easy

Approx time to walk: One hour, but do allow plenty of time for refreshments and sight-seeing

Stiles: One

Map: OS Explorer 190: Malvern Hills and Bredon Hill

Path description: Pastureland, woodland, paved roads and tracks, disused railway line

Start Point: Ledbury Railway Station: SO709386; HR8 1AR

Parking: Street parking in vicinity of station

Dog friendly: Route is popular with dog walkers, no livestock

Public Toilets: About halfway around route in Ledbury town centre

Nearest food: A wide range of cafes, pubs and restaurants in Ledbury town centre

2. At the junction, turn right but you might like to read the information board a few metres to the left. As you walk along Green Lane, gaps in the vegetation to your left afford views to the southern end of the Malvern Hills and the obelisk, erected in 1812 on a hill above Eastnor Castle as a monument to various distinguished members of the Somers Cocks family, who owned the Eastnor estate.

Eventually Green Lane starts to descend steeply. As you pass a grassed area on the left, take a moment to sit and look at the view over the town. It is particularly atmospheric at dusk on a clear winter's day. Moving on, Green Lane meets a path coming in from the right at another information board. You should turn left and continue downhill, descending steps into the edge of Ledbury town. Keep going in the same direction and, a few metres past an open entrance into Netherhall, bear left into a narrow path that passes between two high brick walls. At this point the pavement is well above the level of the road. Immediately turn right through an archway in the wall and enter the walled garden where you start to see the black-and-white buildings characteristic of Ledbury. Walk

through the garden and exit at the wrought iron gates. The walk goes to the right but if you are interested to explore the parish church of St Michael and All Angels, detour to the left. This church is one of seven in Herefordshire to have a bell tower separate from the main building. Walking down the narrow cobbled Church Lane brings you past the Butchers Row Museum, the Heritage Centre and eventually to the Market House,

Ledbury's most famous building. Emerging from Church Lane, you are in the shadow of the Market House in Ledbury town centre – time to patronise one of the many cafes, pubs or restaurants.

3. Continuing the walk, cross the main road by the signal-controlled crossing a few metres to the right of the Market House. Turn left and after a few metres turn right into Bye Street. As you pass the entrance to St Katherine's car park on the left, you may like to go in and view the Master's House, built in the late 15th century for the master of the neighbouring St Katherine's Almshouses. Staying on Bye Street, cross Lawnside leading to Ledbury swimming pool and proceed along a lane running between a row of houses and the black-and-white Brewery Inn.

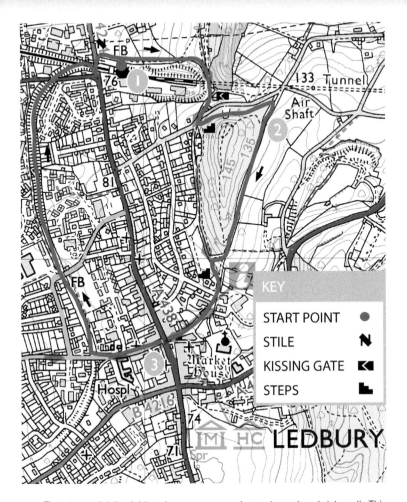

KEY

START POINT	●
STILE	N
KISSING GATE	◄◙
STEPS	◢

LEDBURY

Then bear slightly right and cross a grassed area towards a brick wall. This was the site of the Ledbury Town Halt on the railway from Ledbury station to Gloucester which was closed to passengers in 1959. Turn right to follow the old railway line, which was opened as a footpath in the 1990s and forms part of the Ledbury Town Trail. The trail runs along the side of the recreation ground where there are opportunities for children to play and adults to test out the open-air exercise equipment. Eventually the trail leaves the park behind and crosses a road on a very narrow bridge and becomes tree-lined. Follow the trail, which eventually swings to the right and meets the road. Ledbury Station is once again in sight and you have completed the walk.

QUEENSWOOD COUNTRY PARK

IF YOU GO DOWN IN THE WOODS TODAY YOU'RE SURE TO HAVE A SURPRISE! THIS SHORT WALK INTRODUCES YOU TO SOME OF THE LOVELY THINGS YOU CAN FIND IN THESE WOODS.

Queenswood Country Park is managed by the Herefordshire Council Countryside Service in partnership with the Queenswood Coronation Fund. There are four marked trails and a host of other information boards to add to your pleasure as you walk round. It is a place you can come back to time and time again on your own or with your family and friends. A leaflet about the woods is available from the National Trust shop on site and there is a picnic area and children's adventure playground, toilet facilities and a cafe all adjacent to the large car park.

The top part of Queenswood is an arboretum and contains a collection of specialist trees and a large variety of wild flowers. Around the sides of the hill are 100 acres of semi-natural ancient woodland. This is a fragment of the vast oak wood here which belonged to the Kings of England during the Middle Ages. During the First World War the whole area was felled to provide timber for the war effort. Following this the site was purchased by the Council for the Preservation of Rural England who gave it to the County Council 'for the enjoyment of the public for all time'. The planting of the arboretum began in 1953 when Sir Richard Cotterell, a neighbouring landowner, established the Queenswood Coronation Fund to raise money for the purchase of rare and beautiful trees. You can 'adopt a tree' or simply donate to the fund to help maintain this delightful area.

This walk is an introduction to the wood and its beauty. It is full of interesting features and the flowers and foliage change with the seasons, making the woods a wonderful place to be at any time of the year. The wooden sculptures that you will see were created by local chainsaw carvers. The animals come from woodlands around the world.

The walk starts between the two old buildings at the back of the main car park. To the left is the café, which originally stood as the Essex Arms in Widemarsh Street, Hereford. To the right are the National Trust shop and toilet facilities which are housed in what was once the Tannery building in Leominster.

THE BASICS

Distance: 1½ miles (2.4 km)

Gradient: Gently undulating

Severity: Easy

Approx time to walk: 1 hour

Stiles: None

Map: OS Explorer 202: Leominster and Bromyard

Path description: Maintained woodland paths with some muddy sections

Start Point: Outside the door of the cafe at Queenswood Country Park: SO 506514; HR6 0PY

Parking: Free car park at the entrance to the Country Park

Dog friendly: Dogs on lead in picnic area and under control elsewhere. Please clear up after your dog and use the bins provided

Public Toilets: Yes, by the National Trust shop

Nearest food: Cafe on site

1. Walk ahead and look up as you pass through the archway to see a huge sculpture of a lesser horseshoe bat. They do hang upside down to sleep but really they are only plum sized! Continue ahead along Lime Avenue and later opposite the picture map on the right, bear left along Jubilee Drive.

2. At the junction of several main paths turn sharp right to go back along Nutts Ride and later turn left just at the road to go through a gate into the Autumn Garden.

3. Go through the gate to leave the Autumn Garden. Further on you will notice scots pine each side of path. These are known as Cotterell's Folly and were planted before 1945 to mark the top of the hill. Continue to walk ahead through Oak Avenue. Look at the leaves to distinguish the varieties, there is English, sessile, cork and daimyo oak which has giant leaves (16 by 8 inches or 40 by 20cm).

4. Follow the path across a grassed area surrounded by some more pine trees then just after leaving the grassed area take a small path on the left which goes towards a seat. Do not walk past the owl but continue on the small path as it goes slightly uphill. On reaching the main path turn right and follow it all the way down to the view point.

5. After enjoying the extensive panorama of Herefordshire from the Malvern Hills right round to Garway Hill and Skirrid rejoin the path (with the view point behind you) and go on to the right.

6. At the junction of several paths keep straight ahead (ignore the left turning marked badger trail) and then turn left to follow the deer trail (orange deer print sign) down past the summer garden. This area is left open and uncut in summer for wildflowers, insects and butterflies. Here is a "giant" dormouse.

7. Continue to follow the deer trail. At the 'T' junction with Sovereign Walk sign to your left, continue to your right along Sovereign Walk for a short way . There is a less well defined path off Sovereign Walk to the right – take this – there

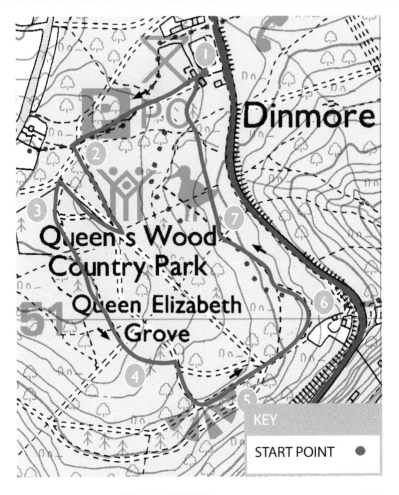

Dinmore

Queen's Wood Country Park

Queen Elizabeth Grove

KEY

START POINT ●

are some tall pine trees on your left. Directly ahead look out for the Deer Trail sign and follow the Deer Trail into the Redwood Grove. Avoiding the muddy patches go up to the left amongst the trees and before you meet the main track take care to find the black bear and don't miss its baby up the tree! Then go up onto the main track and follow it right back to the starting point.

BISHOPSWOOD & BULLS HILL

BISHOPSWOOD IS A VERY SCATTERED VILLAGE MOSTLY HIDDEN FROM THE VALLEY BY THE SHAPE OF THE HILL AND BY TREES.

This walk explores some of the numerous old paths and tracks which served – and still do – the many cottages and agricultural holdings, as well as lime kilns, mills, quarries and coppices. In the Middle Ages the woods belonged to the Bishop of Hereford and were used for hunting and timber. Later, woodsmen will have continually cut and regenerated the trees, managing a very slow controlled burn or charring process on site, to produce charcoal. This was used (before coal) for smelting iron from local ore deposits. As the Industrial Revolution progressed the raw materials changed to coal from the Forest of Dean and low-quality cast iron bars (pig iron) brought up the river by barge and melted again to produce better quality metal.

The railway and station came in 1873 to the area between the car parks and the scenic Kerne Bridge (built as a toll bridge around 1830). Tolls were ended in the mid 1950s. Passenger trains ceased in 1959, and goods trains a few years later.

This is a beautiful walk at all times of year. It has a slightly mysterious air because, despite many traces of past rural and industrial activity, it is hard for us to imagine what life can have been like when it was noisy, smoky and smelly. Spring visitors to the ancient woods will find stunning carpets of wood anemone, bluebell and wild garlic.

THE WALK

1.   Leave the car park by the narrow path in the corner by the parish noticeboard. This leads out to the bus shelter. Cross the main road and walk up the minor road opposite. After passing Glen Kerne house on the right look for a footpath sign on the left, pointing up the access drive to Prospect House and Coombe Lodge. Walk up the drive and carry straight on beside the entrance to Coombe Lodge, taking the path alongside the garden fence.

2.   Your path soon levels out and runs at the top of a steep wooded bank through old woodland of beech, oak, holly, cherry and sweet chestnut. Further along

the forest trees are on both sides. There are glimpses of the River Wye below you. A large rock on the left edge of the path may have rolled down from quarrying activity above. It looks like coarse concrete but is in fact a natural rock called a conglomerate. This very hard, rough rock was traditionally used locally to make mill stones for crushing cider apples to a pulp. You will emerge from the forest at Cherry Tree Cottage.

3. Turn left down the road until you come to a junction just before the main road. Turn right along the concrete track signposted Spring Herne, then keep straight ahead on a gravel track. The past importance of this old cart track through the woodland is indicated by the quality of stretches of still surviving retaining wall along its upper side – although it has been tumbled in places by badgers excavating their setts. Ignore a stile on the left and follow the level narrower path. On the left is a view of Walford Church. Soft fruit and asparagus are grown on the flood plain fields.

4. Cross a concrete drive and carry straight on along the footpath opposite, alongside the wall. Pass by steps on the left as another path joins from across the fields. When you come to a tarmac road turn right, passing Belle Vue on the left and Fair View on the right. You will come to a stone barn on the right-hand side of the lane with a post box set in the wall.

THE BASICS

Distance: 3.8 miles (6.1 km)
Gradient: A hilly walk but without any severe slopes, up or down
Severity: Requires reasonable fitness and mobility
Approx time to walk: 3 hours
Stiles: Two
Map: OS Outdoor Leisure 14: Wye Valley and Forest of Dean (N.B. Bishopswood is shown as Kerne Bridge)
Description: Mostly farm tracks and rougher, old tracks in woodland
Start Point: Free car park to the right of the 'canoe launch', and adjacent to Bishopswood village hall car park: SO581188; HR9 5QT
Parking: See start point
Dog Friendly: Suggest keep on leads especially near houses
Public Toilets: None on route
Nearest food: The Inn on the Wye, Bishopswood

5. Directly opposite this is a tight left turn up a track. Follow this track until it bends left into a house garden. Look for a narrow opening to a path on the right-hand side of this bend. Once you are a few metres up this path you will find that it is a secretive old, narrow sunken way.

6. A couple of hundred metres further on the corner of a wall juts into the line of the path. Watch out because this marks a junction of two paths and you need to turn right, up the less obvious one. This leads you uphill with the wall on your left and then along the outside wall of a house. Carry straight on uphill on a track between high hedgerows with the fields on either side.

7. Where the track comes to a junction with a tarmac road turn left (with your back to Stubbs Cottage). After passing 'Shop Farm Barn' the road goes round a corner to the right and a track goes off to the left. However, you need to take the narrow path ahead (to the left of a wooden transmission pole). After about 100 metres, where the path swings left, turn right along another  narrow path. You will see a stile a few metres ahead. Cross the stile.

8. You emerge from woodland onto the hilltop plateau and the path now runs between a hedge and the fence of a horse riding establishment with open views of the Forest of Dean. Cross another stile, and then cross the road to the track opposite. Go down the track for about 40 metres and turn right onto the concrete drive of Chadwyns Farm. Go straight ahead between the house and farm buildings and on to the grassy path ahead. Bear right through the pedestrian gate and follow the grassy path between hedgerows and for about half a mile (just under 1 km) until you reach a road.

9. Turn right up the road for about 160 metres. Just before a bend look for a path leading sharply back to the left between wooden half-barriers. Take this path, which leads through a plantation of mixed broadleaved trees – a planted-up former small agricultural holding. Bear left slightly as you pass a quirky wooden bench. You will see a barrier and barns ahead.

10. Pass through the barrier and between the two barns. Immediately afterwards turn right along the track. Look through gateways on the left for views across the Wye to Coppet Hill. The track curves to the left – ignore waymarked tracks leading off to the right. At the gateway to Teagues Point leave the track to go

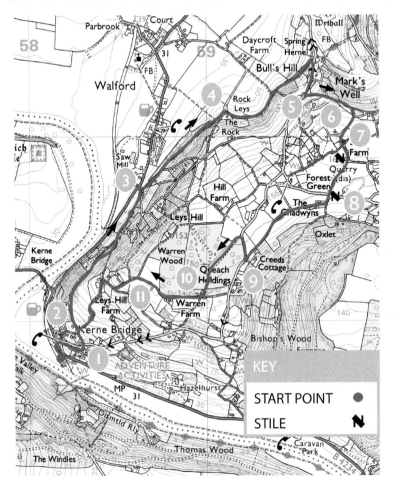

KEY

START POINT ●

STILE ➤

down the narrow sunken path to the left of the gateway. Take care:the going is rough at first.

11. When you reach the bottom of the path turn right along the track, then left along the tarmac between the houses. After about 100 metres turn right down a path past a post with Wye Valley Walk waymarkers. The path winds its way downhill and joins your outward route. Turn left along the drive, then right down the road to the main road and car park.

N.B. To visit the Inn on the Wye use the footpath waymarked in the car park. This is much safer than trying to walk round the blind bend in the main road: there is no pavement or verge.

MERRIVALE

ROSS-ON-WYE IS ONE OF THE FIVE MARKET TOWNS OF HEREFORDSHIRE. ROSS WAS THE BIRTHPLACE OF BRITISH TOURISM.

Overlooking the River Wye, the ancient market town has attracted visitors since the 18th century, who came to escape the industry of the cities and enjoy the scenic Wye Valley and its surrounding countryside. Local tourism began when the rector, Dr John Egerton, started taking friends on boat trips along the river to enjoy the local scenery, castles and abbey. In 1782, William Gilpin's book, Observations on the River Wye was published – the first illustrated tour guide of its kind in Britain. Ross-on-Wye is, to this day, still an excellent base for those wishing to explore the Wye Valley and Forest of Dean. In Ross-on-Wye itself, the visitor will find plenty to do and many old buildings of historic interest, including the parish church of St Mary's, Ross Market Building (now the Heritage Centre) and many more. Ross-on-Wye is also a great place for walkers. Along with Bromyard, Kington and Leominster it is one of Herefordshire's four 'Walkers are Welcome' towns and there is a great selection of walks, short or long, in the area.

This is a short walk to stretch the legs and enjoy the steep wooded hill that provides a backdrop to the market town of Ross-on-Wye. You can drive to the start, or easily walk the half-mile (less than a kilometre) out from the town centre. The route climbs and then traverses the saddle of the wooded hill overlooking the town. The return section uses the former Wye Valley Railway Line, a track now used by walkers and cyclists which forms part of the Ross Town Trail.

THE BASICS

Distance: 2 miles (3 km)

Gradient: Generally fairly easy, but there is a long uphill section at the start

Severity: A leisurely country walk

Approx time to walk: 1½ hours

Stiles: None

Map: Either OS Explorer 189 (Hereford and Ross-on-Wye) or Outdoor Leisure 14 (Wye Valley and Forest of Dean)

Description: Firm tracks, pastureland and unsurfaced woodland paths

Start point: Car park at Fernbank Road (almost at junction with Eastfield Road): SO597231; HR9 5PP

Parking: Free car park

Dogs: Dog friendly, but keep on leads especially on Fernbank Road and in the fields (cows, horses and sheep)

Public Toilets: None on the route

Nearest food: Great selection of pubs, cafes and restaurants in the town

MERRIVALE WALK

1. From the car park head up the road past all the houses. The road becomes a stone track. As you reach the top of the track you will approach the buildings of Hill Farm. A few metres before the farm buildings there is a gravel parking/ loading area on the left. Go around any parked vehicles and in the back corner of the parking area you will find a path through the bushes leading a few metres down to a half-hidden wooden kissing gate.

2. Go through the kissing gate into the wood and follow the path that curves to the right, ignoring other woodland paths that lead off to the left. After about 300 metres you will come to the corner of the wood beside a stone memorial bench and kissing gate.

3. Go through the gate and follow the fence on your right along the top side of a grassy field.

4. Ahead there is a gap leading to the next field but instead of passing through the gap look for a 'Wye Valley Walk' marker immediately to the left of the gap and follow the small path into the trees. The path soon widens and further on becomes an old sunken way. Follow this gently downhill until you reach a gate. Go through the gate, and immediately cross over a path and go through another small gate and out into a field. This is the field local people use for sledging – using anything that will slide on snow! Although you could take a short cut down the steep slope you would miss a view of the town and the steeple of St Mary's Church.

5. Walk to the right (uphill) of the aerial mast enclosure that lies immediately ahead of you. Follow the grassy path all around the edge of the field until you reach a metal gate where the path goes back into the wood at the bottom of the steep slope.

6. Take the path through the wood, bearing right through an old metal kissing gate where the path divides either side of a derelict fence. You will emerge through

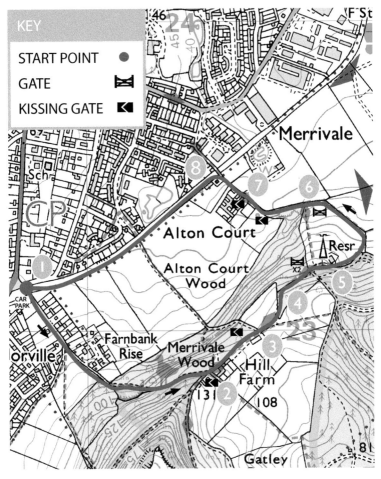

another kissing gate onto a tarmac road in front of Alton Court, a beautiful black-and-white building which is the national headquarters of PGL (adventure holidays for children).

7.   Go down the road. Watch for the lion-headed gateposts of a house on the left and turn left up a tarmac path just after the house.

8.   After a few yards the path becomes a straight and level gravel track. This is actually the trackbed of the old Ross to Monmouth railway line, which was finally closed in 1968. Walk all the way along the track, which eventually zigzags up out of a deep rock cutting to emerge in Fernbank Road car park

ROSS-ON-WYE TO WESTON UNDER PENYARD

THIS LINEAR WALK STARTS IN THE TOWN CENTRE AND PASSES SOME OF THE TOWN'S BEST HISTORICAL LANDMARKS AND VIEWPOINTS ON THE WAY TO MERRIVALE WOOD AND THE VILLAGE OF WESTON UNDER PENYARD.

The return bus stop is conveniently opposite the Weston Cross Inn and there is a regular service back to Ross-on-Wye. (N.B. There are no buses on Sundays.)

Ross-on-Wye is an old market town close to the border with Gloucestershire and Monmouthshire (Wales). It lies beside one of the tight bends in the River Wye and originally derived its wealth from being a river traffic trading point and later from road traffic once a bridge was built across the river at Wilton.

Merrivale Wood and the adjoining Chase and Penyard woods cover the hills that provide the lovely backdrop to the old market town. Merrivale Wood is an attractive ancient woodland at all times of year. It contains several sandstone outcrops including an old quarry. The quarry is fenced at the top but is not far from the path, so take care with children.

The footpaths in the woods are sometimes narrow in places, with roots and rocks to watch for in the path. While looking out for the wild flowers, rabbits and deer you will probably also spot the badger setts at the bottom of Merrivale Wood. You may also see where grassy areas in fields and beside paths have been grubbed up by the wild boar that have become established in this part of Herefordshire. (Quietly take a detour in the unlikely event that you actually come across wild boar.)

THE BASICS

Distance: 3½ miles (6 km)

Gradient: Moderate: slopes up & down throughout the walk* (Alternative route available)

Severity: Moderate. Requires reasonable fitness and mobility

Approx min. time to walk: 3 hours

Stiles: One

Map: Either OS Explorer 189 (Hereford and Ross-on-Wye) or Outdoor Leisure 14 (Wye Valley and Forest of Dean)

Description: Town and country road and tracks, pastureland and (potentially slippery) unsurfaced woodland paths

Start Point: Market Hall in the centre of Ross-on-Wye: SO599241; HR9 5HE

End Point: Weston under Penyard: SO631233; HR9 7NU. (** Return details)

Parking: Various long-stay car parks or street parking in town

Dogs: Dog friendly, but keep on leads especially on Fernbank Road and in the fields

Public Toilets: The Croft Centre

Nearest food: Great selection of pubs, cafes and restaurants in the town

ROSS-ON-WYE WALK (LINEAR)

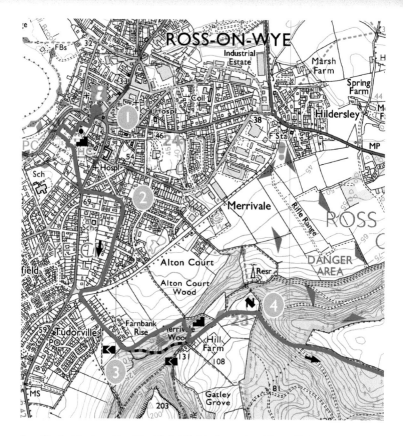

1. Start at the top side of the Market Hall in the centre of town. With your back to the Market Hall you will be looking at an old black-and-white building with a plaque commemorating John Kyrle, 'The Man of Ross', a major benefactor to the town. Go to your right along the narrow one-way High Street and take the first turn on the left into Church Street. To your left you pass some very old almshouses (originally a 14th-century hospital converted to houses for the poor and restored in 1575 – and again recently!). Climb up the steps on your right into the churchyard of St Mary's. At the top of the steps you will see the old Plague Cross commemorating the burial nearby of 317 people without coffins in the Plague of 1637. Cross the churchyard past the church porch then bear left to take the path to the side of the church. After a few yards turn right through a pillared entrance to a little park, 'The Prospect'. Walk over to the railings to admire the view. When the river is in flood the park and fields below you are under water between the old town bridge on your left and the modern bridge on the dual carriageway on your right, reaching the top of the steps at the Rowing Club near that bridge. The remains of Wilton Castle can be seen on the opposite bank, near the old bridge. The Prospect was a gift to

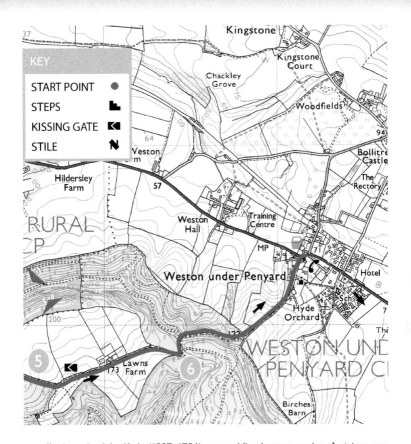

KEY

START POINT ●

STEPS ▚

KISSING GATE ◪

STILE ◣

the town by John Kyrle (1637–1724) as a public pleasure garden. A cistern was installed in the Prospect in 1705 to store water pumped up from the river by pumps powered by a waterwheel. Wooden pipes carried the water from the cistern to taps around the town. Leave The Prospect through the John Kyrle gateway erected in 1700. Steps take you down into the cemetery. Turn left along by the wall and head for the cemetery exit straight ahead. Turn right though the car park and along the path between the Bowling Club and tennis courts to a road junction. Cross the minor roads to the front of the Prince of Wales pub, then cross the main road at the traffic lights and turn right along the pavement. Turn into the first turning on the left: The Avenue. Go down the avenue of lime trees and then right at the bottom into Eastfield Road.

2.   Walk along Eastfield Road. Pass the ends of Merrivale Road and Merrivale Crescent, go round a bend to the right and turn left into Fernbank Road on your left, just before a play park. Head up Fernbank Road past all the houses. The road becomes a stone track.

3. Look out for a wooden kissing gate on the left and go through the gate into the Merrivale Wood Nature Reserve. (N.B. An alternative Route is available to avoid the rough and sometimes slippery stepped climb ahead! See Note at end of the main description). Take the undulating path along the bottom of the wood. After about 350 metres look for a stepped path on the right leading uphill. Take the steps and bear left where another path comes in from the right. Continue upwards through the wood and turn left along the track at the top (waymarked 'Wye Valley Walk'). The track soon emerges at the edge of the wood beside

   a stone memorial bench and kissing gate. Go through the gate and walk along by the fence of the two fields ahead. There is a lovely valley to your right and a view of the northern fringe of the Forest of Dean. Look behind you for a marvellous view across the Herefordshire hills to the Black Mountains of Wales. Cross the stile at top corner of the field. Walk up the gravel path from the stile to join a track a few metres inside the wood. Turn right along the track. It curves gradually to the left and climbs gently.

4. After about 300 metres you will be approaching the top of the rise where the track bends slightly to the right. Just before the bend look for a narrow path

   leading off to the left through the bushes. Take this path, which after about 70 yards passes in front of a metal gate and continues along the line of a fence. Go to the right of the gate and continue along the path with the fence on your left. The path stays in the wood but soon has a field on the other side. There are little diversions from the line of the fence to avoid obstructions but be sure always to come back out to this wood edge path as soon as you can. Ahead and slightly to the left there is a view of May Hill with its distinctive clump of trees on top. After about 600 metres the fence path comes to a gate at the corner of the wood.

5. Go through the gate and immediately turn left along the top of the grassy field. This public footpath leads along the top of the fields to Lawns Farm – you will soon see the buildings ahead. Please keep dogs on leads as requested. Carry

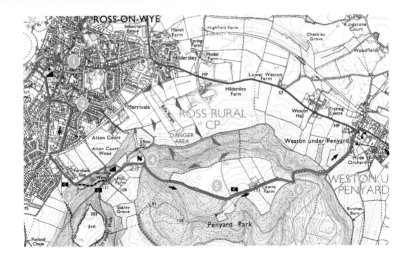

on though a kissing gate, passing to the right of the farm buildings. Here you join the farm access track, which soon drops downhill and runs just inside the woodland fence with a field on the right. Follow the track as it curves slightly to the right. You will soon come to a T-junction of tracks.

6. Turn left and follow the track downhill. Make sure to keep right at a fork after 100 metres. Stay on this track all the way down the hill to the village of Weston under Penyard. As you exit the wood you will see the church ahead. Walk down the lane passing the church until you emerge at the busy A40 main road opposite the Weston Cross Inn. The bus stop shelter is to your right.

Alternative route at the entrance to Merrivale Wood Nature Reserve...

Carry on up the track. As you reach the top of the hill you will approach the buildings of Hill Farm. A few metres before the farm buildings there is a gravel parking/loading area on the left. Go around any parked vehicles and in the back corner of the parking area you will find a path through the bushes leading a few yards down to a half-hidden a wooden kissing gate. Go through the kissing gate into the wood and follow the path that curves to the right, ignoring other paths off to the left. After about 300 metres you will come to the corner of the wood beside a stone memorial bench and kissing gate. Here you rejoin the main route.

* There is a steeper, roughly stepped path in Merrivale Wood.
** Return bus number; 33 from Weston under Penyard (NOT SUNDAYS). Ring Traveline on 0871 200 2233 for details.

THE BLACK HILL

The Black Hill is the most mountainous part of Herefordshire on the eastern side of the Black Mountains.

The trig point at 640 metres (2,100 feet) is the highest point in this book. The Black Hill is also known as the 'Cat's Back'. If approaching from the east towards the Black Mountains the shape of the hill appears like the back of a hunched, sitting cat. This is probably the most ambitious walk in this book but your efforts will be rewarded with the most stunning views in all directions, and a wonderful experience of the wide open spaces of the Welsh border.

This area is at times subject to low cloud. In these conditions, unless you are an experienced mountain walker with appropriate equipment, simply turn back and enjoy whatever view you have. It can also be extremely windy on top. On a fine day it is as well to take sun cream and a hat as most of the walk is without tree cover.

*The easiest way to the Black Hill is to follow the A465 to Pandy, then turn north at the Pandy Inn and follow the road signposted to Longtown. Continuing past the remains of Longtown Castle, the road then becomes a single-track road with frequent passing places. At the next two junctions, follow the first sign (left) indicating the Black Hill and the second sign indicating the picnic area (straight on). Continue along the road for ¾ mile (1 km) and turn right up a steep hill to the picnic site.

THE BASICS

Distance: 5 miles (8 km)

Gradient: One short steep climb at the start and one fairly steep descent

Severity: Energetic

Approx min time to walk: 3 hours

Stiles: None

Maps: OS Explorer Outdoor Leisure 13: Brecon Beacons (Eastern area)

Path description: Stony or grass paths with a lane to finish. Some rocky sections to be taken carefully

Start point: Black Hill car park; see note on opposite page for location of car park*

Parking: Black Hill car park (12 cars); SO288327; HR2 0NL

Dog friendly: Dogs will need to be on leads much of the walk because of sheep and ponies

Public Toilets: None

Nearest food: The Crown Inn, Longtown; Bull's Head, Craswall

THE BLACK HILL WALK

1. Walking past the picnic tables go through the gate and follow the path leading straight up the grassy/bracken slope towards the rocky area ahead of you. Take your time and stop to admire the views behind you and to the east. To the west and below you is the Olchlon valley. Above this is Hatterall Ridge where you will see people walking Offa's Dyke. Of further interest is that virtually due west and on the lower west flank of Hatterall Ridge is The Vision, the home of the two brothers described in Bruce Chatwin's famous 1982 book On the Black Hill. The book centres on the lives of Lewis and Benjamin Jones whose lives were led almost entirely around The Vision. Chatwin was a regular visitor to this area from the age of 15 and towards the end of his life often came here to write. There is also a powerful film, with wonderful photography of the area, directed by Andrew Grieve (1987). Continue to walk along the ridge, taking care when crossing or climbing on the rocky outcrops and enjoy the panorama as it unfolds ahead of you. In the springtime  look out for the ponies with their foals. Enjoy the wild flowers, the heather, gorse and, if you are lucky, the paragliders. After about 1½ miles (2 km) from the start you will reach the trig point 640m (2,100 feet) above sea level.

2. From the trig point, walk to the left around the waterlogged area, and continue to follow the track roughly parallel to the ridge in a north-westerly direction. After ¾ mile (1 km) from the trig point look out for a small pile of stones – a crucial marker you mustn't miss!

3. Turn left, almost going back on yourself, now walking south-east along the bridleway which descends with a steeper gradient. Take care when walking over wet patches as you proceed along the track. Enjoy the superb views of the Olchon Valley as you walk. Stop to admire the tumbling stream; however, carefully negotiate the rocky patch of the bridleway beyond the stream. Go down the bridleway until you reach a tree-lined area on your right. Continue close to the fence line until you reach a gate at the edge of a wood. Continue on the

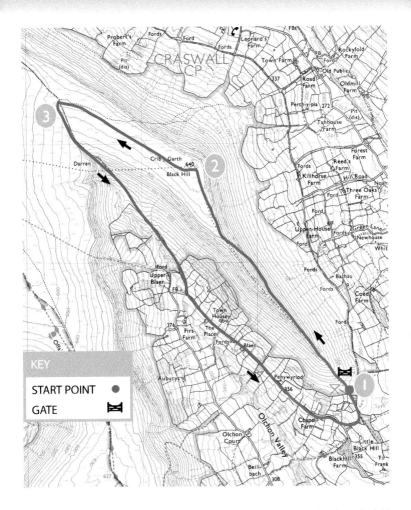

KEY

START POINT ●

GATE

bridleway through the wood until you reach the minor road. Continue straight on, along the road, and note the now derelict moss-covered farm buildings which continue along this road into Llanveynoe. These indicate a time of an active population at Upper Bleun which existed over hundreds of years, and the importance of these tracks during that period. Continue walking along the tree-lined road, admiring the local views until you reach the turning on the left taking you up the steep incline to where the cars are parked. If you want to extend your day, you could visit Llanveynoe Church or Longtown Castle – or you could repair to one of the local pubs (but do check opening times beforehand).

WEOBLEY

THE VILLAGE OF WEOBLEY DATES BACK TO MEDIEVAL TIMES, WHEN IT WAS A PROSPEROUS MARKET TOWN AND WOOL TRADING CENTRE.

Its isolation and lack of development has ensured that many of its timber-framed buildings have remained virtually intact over the centuries, providing the village with a rich heritage of such historic properties.

Weobley is an idyllic place to visit and forms part of Herefordshire's 'Black and White Village Trail'. The village contains its own Heritage Trail, with information plaques placed at appropriate points, which explain the various historic buildings and their architectural features. A map of the village is provided by the parking area in Bell Square, the starting point of the walk. This shows the locations of the information plaques and relates a brief history of Weobley. You can also visit the remains of an 11th-century castle and a 12th-century church which has the second highest tower in the county. There are a number of shops in the village and refreshments are available at excellent inns and tearooms.

This picturesque village lies in the heart of Herefordshire's rich agricultural pastureland, surrounded by rolling hills and beautiful countryside. The circular walking route uses quiet lanes and firm paths across fields to the hamlet of Ledgemoor. Here it is possible to visit the Marshpools Country Inn. The return to Weobley includes some of the Garnstone Estate's Conservation Walks and crosses the Castle Green into the village. The scenery is delightful throughout the walk.

THE BASICS

Distance: 3½ miles (6 km)

Gradient: Minimal

Severity: Easy

Approx min. time to walk: 2 hours

Stiles: One

Map: OS Explorer 202: Leominster and Bromyard

Path description: Village lanes and firm field tracks

Start point: Weobley public car park, off B4230: SO401517; HR4 8SE

Parking: As above

Dog friendly: Yes, but keep dogs on leads on pastureland

Public Toilets: By the museum in Weobley, off B4230

Nearest food: Weobley village has shops, inns, a restaurant and tea rooms
Marshpools Inn is near the midpoint of the walk

WEOBLEY WALK

1. Leaving the car park turn left and then right, just beyond the Red Lion, to go up Broad Street past the centre of the village with its shops and interesting magpie sculpture at the top. Turn left at the top to pass the Unicorn Inn and, ignoring the right turn to Hereford, continue straight on to pass the Dental Surgery/Parish Council noticeboard and then a house called 'The Sallies' on the right. Just after this house, take the paved lane on the right. This becomes a green lane which you follow, bearing left to ignore paths coming from the right, until you reach a kissing gate which you go through into a field.

2. Go diagonally left across the field through a gap in the trees to a gate in the left hedge. Follow the track diagonally right across the next field to a gate which gives onto a tarmac road. Cross the road and follow a green lane opposite which leads to a gate (usually open) and a waymark sign. The path across the next complex of fields is clear and well signed. Walk the right-hand edge of the first two fields and go through a gate into a large field. Follow the well-defined pathway straight on across this and two further large fields. In the third field the path leads slightly to the right to an oak tree ahead, and to the left, a detached red-brick house and a nearby telephone kiosk with a union jack-painted roof. Cross the step stile under the oak tree into the tarmac lane.

3. Turn right and follow the lane to take a turning on the left to the Marshpools Inn. Head towards the inn, ignoring the turning on the left. About 50 metres before the Inn, near a white-painted house, is a footpath on the right. If you visit the Inn come back to this point and take this path across the field to a tarmac lane. Turn right and follow the lane to a junction with a tall wellingtonia tree at the corner where you turn left. Follow this lane and continue to a T-junction with the Hereford Road.

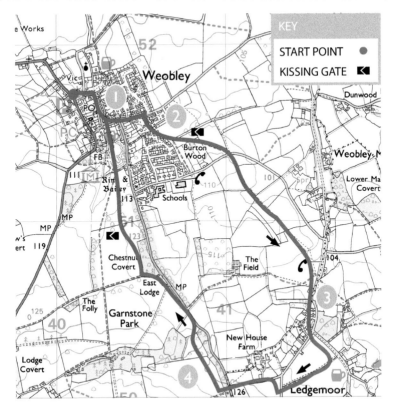

4.   Turn left for 50 metres, then right into the entrance to a Garnstone Estate farm track which leads onto one of the Garnstone Estate's conservation walks. Go through a pedestrian gate on the left and turn sharp right to walk down the side of a long copse. At the far end of the copse turn right to go out onto the Hereford Road again. Take care as the Hereford Road can be busy. Go left and follow the road for about 400 metres, passing a lodge, to another entrance to the Garnstone Estate. Turn left into this entrance and follow the estate road to a gateway by a copse. Turn right and follow the path alongside the hedge and then a wire fence on your right to a kissing gate in a corner of the field. Go through the gate and go straight ahead across the large field, returning to the village via Castle Green.

Top: Bromyard Downs © Visit Herefordshire
Bottom: Fishing On Wye © Visit Herefordshire

Top: Golden Valley © Visit Herefordshire
Bottom: Cathedral Bridge © Visit Herefordshire

ABOUT THE AUTHORS

HEREFORDSHIRE RAMBLERS.

This book is the work of numerous members of Herefordshire Ramblers. Between us we have researched, walked and checked all the walks in this book. If you enjoy walking, we hope you will think about joining the Ramblers.

Thanks are due to all who helped with this book, Tom Fisher, Eileen Garvey, Isobel Gibson, Mike Goodwin, David Hawkins, Mary Howcroft, Pam Johnson, Howard Jones, Jenny Jones, Marika Kovaks, Arthur Lee, Sally Northcott, Bob Selmes, Wendy Sladen and Mary Woodage.

The Ramblers is Britain's largest walking charity, which was formed in 1935 to promote walking and to campaign for better access to the countryside. Locally Herefordshire Ramblers organises a wide variety of led walks, from short to long, all across the county and beyond. All are welcome.

Look us up on our website at www.herefordshireramblers.org.uk.

We look forward to seeing you.